CULTURE SHOCK!

Chile

Susan Roraff
Laura Camacho

K·U·P·E·R·A·R·D

In the same series

Australia	Indonesia	Philippines	A Parent's Guide
Bolivia	Ireland	Singapore	A Traveller's Medical Guide
Britain	Israel	South Africa	A Wife's Guide
California	Italy	Spain	Living and Working Abroad
Canada	Japan	Sri Lanka	Living & Working in London
China	Korea	Sweden	Living & Working in Paris
Cuba	Laos	Switzerland	Living & Working in Rome
Czech	Malaysia	Syria	Working Holidays Abroad
Republic	Mauritius	Taiwan	
Denmark	Mexico	Thailand	
Egypt	Morocco	Turkey	
France	Myanmar	UAE	
Germany	Nepal	USA	
Greece	Netherlands	USA—The	
Hong Kong	Norway	South	
India	Pakistan	Vietnam	

Culture Shock! Chile
First published in Great Britain 1998 by
Kuperard
No 7 Spectrum House
32-34 Gordon House Road
London NW5 1LP

Kuperard is an imprint of Bravo Ltd.

Illustrations by TRIGG
Cover photographs from Topham Picture Point

Printed in Singapore

ISBN ! 85733-239-3

This book is dedicated to our husbands Enrique and Patricio for all their love and support.

CONTENTS

PREFACE

So you're a foreigner living in Chile. Congratulations on selecting (or having had the luck to be sent to) one of the preferred destinations in all of South America. While every country has its charms, the great majority of our Latin American, North American and European friends would move to Chile in a heartbeat given the opportunity.

Nevertheless, we are sure that at times living in Chile will be difficult – no one ever said expatriate life was a bed of roses. Living abroad strips away many of the things that before had helped to define ourselves – our language, family, friends and culture. We are left standing naked in a strange land and must fight to determine the boundaries of our very being. Yet there are strategies for survival. Experts say that those with an interest in the host country adjust better. So take up a hobby! Collect Chilean minerals, visit every volcano, ski slope or beach in all of Chile, learn Spanish well enough to read Chile's two Nobel prize winners, volunteer to work with the needy, birdwatch, anything to convince yourself that Chile is the best place to be at this moment.

It is of the utmost importance that you find a social support network. Socializing with those living in your home does not count. Work or study has been found to be very comforting to those living abroad, as the rhythmic schedule and socialization buffer cultural stress. If you do not work outside the home, making friends is a matter of life or death. You can go to your embassy to find out about clubs, associations, etc. involving expatriates from your own country, or at least your language group. The experts say it is best not to become too involved in your fellow citizen's activities, but that's easy for them to say! The circumstances are a better guide in our opinion. If you have transferred with your whole family and only plan to stay in Chile for a year, then the comfort of expatriate friends is more than reasonable. Expatriates tend to form intense friendships very quickly, as they need the mutual social support. But we also know people in denial, who marry foreigners, speak only English (even after 10 years abroad) and have only expatriate friends. They dream of returning to their home country, but know that this will not happen. This is not a healthy situation.

Spanish is an absolute must for anyone on more than a vacation. Integration into your host society may seem at first like the death of your old identity, but in the long run you can become an extraordinary person who is a full member of the society in which you live. Actually, most people we know who have lived in Chile eventually learned to speak passable Spanish, worked or studied, had many Chilean friends and generally integrated into Chilean society without too much difficulty. It is common to go "deep" into Chile and associate mostly with Chileans.

Do not think that the person who passes through customs on his or her way "home" someday will be the same person who arrived in Chile. People evolve, and Chile will affect you in many ways. It is typical for friends and relatives back home to see the same person that they knew before, but in reality, after a time you may start seeing even your homeland through Chilean eyes. For example, an American girlfriend of ours became more conscious of class structures and tended to identify with the lower classes during her stay in Chile. Upon returning home she was distressed to realize that "Everyone's *cuico!*" (an upper class snob).

In this day and age it is not uncommon to live for extended periods abroad, but that does not mean that it is uncomplicated. Most people put up a brave facade, but privately many things about their new environment are unexplainable (or so it seems), unreasonable or just plain stupid. It is easy for foreigners to commit a faux pas without knowing the reason for their blunder. It is our goal to explain how and why Chile is the way it is, with the ultimate objective of making your stay in Chile, whether long or short, as pleasant as possible. Fore-warned is forearmed!

CHILE

— *Chapter One* —

THE SPINE OF SOUTH AMERICA

GEOGRAPHICAL OVERVIEW

Physical geography and climate are perhaps the first of many differences that a foreigner encounters while living abroad. Odds are that the landscape, the flora and fauna, even the air you breathe in Chile will not be the same as those from your place of reference. Depending on your point of view, these differences may be the most difficult to overcome, or the easiest to adapt to. In any case, Chile offers a variety of scenery that is hard to match.

Not the Tropics

When people think of South America, visions of white beaches, palm trees and tropical jungles with monkeys usually come to mind. Some of Latin America actually does fit that description, but not Chile. There may be palm trees, but they have been planted; there are beaches, but you can only sunbathe in season; the hot regions of Chile are far too dry to sustain a jungle and the moist regions are far too cool.

The Longest Country in the World

Chile is most likely very far away from your country of reference. Due to this distance, many people are only familiar with the country's strange geography. Chile is long and thin. Superimposed on a map of the United States, Chile would stretch from northern Maine to southern California. On a map of Europe, Chile would stretch from Moscow to Lisbon. It is 4,270 kilometers (2,647 miles) long, yet averages only 177 kilometers (110 miles) across.

Chile, the longest country in the world, boasts nearly 4,300 kilometers of beautiful coastline.

Chile was founded as a Spanish colony on the western side of the formidable barrier of the Andes Mountains along the coast of the Pacific Ocean. It was easier to expand to the south (into the territories of the indigenous groups) and to the north (into the neglected parts of Peru and Bolivia) than it was to cross these mountains and venture farther inland. Although the Spanish crown originally assigned certain territories beyond the Andes to Chile (in what today is southern Argentina), the country eventually found its "natural" niche between the mountains and the sea.

Geographical Divisions

Although there is a tremendous variety of geography, the country can be divided conveniently into threes. There are three distinct regions moving east to west. Here the major features are the Andes Mountains, the Central Valley and the coastal ranges of the Cordillera de la Costa. These regions run almost perfectly parallel throughout the length of the country.

From north to south Chile can also be divided into three sections. Those familiar with North American geography could compare Chile with the west coast of the continent upside-down. Instead of forests and glaciers in the north, followed by a temperate region, and the deserts of southern California and Mexico, Chile is characterized by deserts in the north, fertile valleys in the center and forests, glaciers and fjords in the south.

The North

Starting in the north, we find the Atacama Desert – one of the driest places in the world. In certain areas rainfall has never been registered, although some vegetation survives on condensation from the fog, or *camanchaca*, that forms over the cold ocean waters. Temperatures are mild, averaging 20.5°C (69°F) in summer and 14°C (57°F) in winter.

Most of the population lives close to the ocean where humidity levels are higher. Since the opening of a new asphalt highway between La Paz and Arica, Bolivian tourists fleeing the cold of the Altiplano regularly vacation at the seaside cities of Arica and Iquique.

The Atacama Desert is also home to geoglyphs, or large drawings made from stones arranged on the sides of mountains. It is said that these interesting archeological relics point the way to the sea. Not far from the village of San Pedro de Atacama and its famous Archeological Museum are the Tatio geysers. These are well worth a visit. Beautiful Lake Chungará is also found in this region, located high in the Altiplano and is home to flamingos (*parinas*). For adventurers, the north also contains remnants of the Camino del Inca, the road the Incas used to maintain the unity of their conquered lands.

The Central Region

Central Chile, where the majority of the population lives, has a Mediterranean climate. It is part of what is known as the Central Valley. This is where rich soils essential for producing fresh fruit, such as grapes used to produce the famous Chilean wines, can be found. Santiago, the capital, is located here.

The South

Chile's world famous Lake District runs from Temuco to Puerto Montt, and includes the island of Chiloé. It is noted for its beautiful scenery, including volcanoes, lakes, forests and rivers. It is one of the biggest tourist destinations in South America. Lago Llanquihue is the second deepest lake in South America (Lake Titicaca is the deepest). The name means "deep place" in Mapuche. On the other side of the Osorno Volcano is the Lago Todos Los Santos. This lake is a brilliant green due to its high mineral content. At the base of the volcano are the Saltos de Petrohué, where volcanic rock has turned the tranquil river into rapids.

The Extreme South

Further south is the Canals Region, where fjords, glaciers and volcanoes can be found. As you travel south the land eventually breaks down into many islands. The Aisén Region has been colonized by a small number of pioneers with the active support of the government. As a result, there are a number of small villages throughout this region. It is a rugged landscape that only a few have been able to conquer. The Austral Highway was constructed to connect this isolated region with the rest of the country. It begins in Puerto Montt and provides some spectacular views. However, it is not an easy drive. It is best undertaken in a four wheel drive vehicle during the summer. And bring your own supply of gasoline and food since neither is readily found along the way.

Torres del Paine National Park just north of Puerto Natales is Chile's most famous national park, known for its unspoiled beauty. No cars are allowed inside the park. For the adventurous there is a 10-day hiking trail circling the park. Camping is popular, but be sure to secure your tent because the winds are fierce and can easily uproot tents. For those who prefer a bed at night there is a hotel at the entrance.

Precipitation

The climatic variation in Chile can best be demonstrated by precipitation levels. Northern Chile receives very little rainfall, while central Chile receives around 305–355 mm (12–14 inches) a year, mostly during the winter months (April–September). Southern Chile receives over 2,300 mm (90 inches) of rain a year, and the islands of western Patagonia receive over 4,100 mm (160 inches) of rain a year! The Nobel Prize winning Chilean poet Pablo Neruda often made mention of the endless rain in his childhood district of Temuco. Southern Chile receives one of the highest amounts of precipitation in the world. In the spring, melting snow from the Andes swells small rivers into powerful ones. Many of these are used as a source of electricity. More than three-fourths of the country's electricity is produced by hydroelectric plants, the rest is generated by thermal plants.

Antarctica

The Chilean Antarctic Territory is roughly the same as the area also claimed by Argentina and Great Britain. While it is included on all Chilean maps, in keeping with the Antarctic Treaty, all claims have been temporarily frozen. Chile established the first of its five scientific and exploration bases there in 1947.

Easter Island

Easter Island (Isla de Pascua in Spanish or Rapa Nui in Polynesian) is the best known of Chile's Pacific islands. It lies 3,700 kilometers (2,300 miles) off the coast of Chile and is considered the most isolated island in the world. The island was called Te Pito O Te Henua (Navel

of the World) by the first settlers, Polynesian travelers who sailed there in bark canoes over 1,500 years ago. Admiral Roggeveen, a Dutchman, gave the island its name when he stumbled upon it on Easter Day in 1722. By 1877, the population had dropped to only 111 people as a result of slavery, disease, war and deforestation. It was annexed by Chile in 1888 and, in effect, became a large sheep ranch.

Easter Island is known for its 867 Moais. These sculptures of volcanic rock, believed to represent deceased chiefs or gods, can stand as tall as 6 meters (20 feet). The Moais attract many foreign tourists, but most Chileans have never been to the island because of the prohibitively high cost. Easter Island's current population numbers around 2,800 and efforts are underway to conserve the native language of the Rapa Nui, which is vanishing as the inhabitants increasingly learn Spanish, French and English for tourism purposes. Since 1965 tourism has become the principal industry.

Islas Juan Fernández

Another group of islands for which Chile is famous is the Islas Juan Fernández, located 587 kilometers (364 miles) west of Valparaíso. You may not be familiar with the name, but one of the islands was where Alexander Selkirk was marooned for about four years. He survived by capturing feral goats, and he dressed in their skins. He later said he was never so happy as when he was alone on this island, which today is called Isla Robinson Crusoe.

Land Usage

Less than one-tenth of Chile's land is arable, almost all of it in the central region. One-sixth of the land is permanent pasture that supports substantial herds of sheep and cattle. A little more than one-tenth is forested. Much of the rest of the country is covered by desert and highlands. National parks account for roughly 18 percent of Chilean territory, a fairly high percentage. CONAF, the National Park Service, runs the 30 or so national parks, reserves and sanctuaries.

FLORA

There are thousands of unique plant species in Chile. The *copihue*, which is found in southern Chile, is the national flower. It is a vine from the lily family that produces a red, white or pink bell-shaped flower. The *alerce* tree, a slow-growing tree found in the south, is noted for its longevity. Some *alerces* are over 4,000 years old. Because the wood is water resistant, many homes in the region are made from these trees and sadly many forests have been depleted. The government is trying to preserve what is left for future generations.

Another beautiful tree seen throughout the central and south central regions is the large and stately *araucaria* tree. At times you may hear indigenous groups referred to as Araucanos, a term derived from the tree native to their homeland.

WILDLIFE

Chile's indigenous wildlife include the alpaca, *vicuña*, llama, puma, the Andean huemul and the Andean cat. During the summer on the Andean plateau, rainfall forms shallow lakes that are home to many bird species, including the Chilean flamingo. The huemul, a large deer, and the Chilean condor are found in great numbers and appear on the national coat of arms. Chilean pumas survive in reduced numbers in national parks in the south. The pumas sporadically kill the sheep and goats raised in the south and the farmers retaliate by hunting them. There are two poisonous spiders in Chile, the *araña del trigo,* generally found in wheat fields, and the *araña de rincón.* You may want to buy a guidebook to help identify these species.

GEOLOGICAL AND CLIMATIC PHENOMENA

Chile is a geologist's dream, not only because of its plethora of minerals, but also because of its fascinating global position. The Nazca Plate, a large section of the Pacific Ocean floor, is moving towards Chile at a rate of 10 centimeters (4 inches) a year, and crashing into the South American continental plate. This movement has caused the formation of the Peru-Chile Trench, just off the coast of northern Chile. The trench is about 150 kilometers (90 miles) wide and averages 5,000 meters (16,500 feet) in depth. The deepest point (8,066 meters, 26,473 feet) is north of Antofagasta. The movement of the Nazca Plate has created the spectacular Andes Mountains, complete with over 620 volcanoes, many of them active. It has also made the region highly prone to earthquakes. If you are interested in seeing nature at work, Oyahue, Socompa and Lastarria are active volcanoes in the north and Llaima and Hudson are in the south.

Earthquakes

In modern times Chile has been struck by 28 earthquakes with a force greater than 6.9 on the Richter scale. In Santiago you may feel tremors every few months depending on the humor of the Nazca Plate. At least one tremor occurs every day somewhere in Chile. The city of Valparaíso has been demolished on half a dozen occasions due to earthquakes. In 1960 quakes struck southern Chile and caused giant tidal waves that swept inland and killed thousands of people. Central Chile shook in March of 1985, killing more than 100 people and leaving thousands homeless.

The Humbolt Current

The Humbolt Current runs the entire length of Chile, tempering the coastal climate. It originates near Antarctica and flows from south to north, a fact with which you will be familiar after visiting one of Chile's many beaches. Even in summer, the water temperature in central Chile only reaches 15°C (59°F). The Humbolt Current veers away from the coast near Antofagasta, so bathers in the northern region enjoy warm waters.

El Niño

In recent years the phenomenon called El Niño has gained worldwide attention. The name, meaning "The Christ Child," was coined by Peruvian fishermen to describe a warm Pacific Ocean current that appeared around Christmas every three to seven years. Western trade winds weaken at this time, and without the winds, the warm waters of the Pacific flow east towards South America. Today scientists have learned that El Niño disrupts global weather patterns. Heavy rains have been known to hit central and northern Chile, normally desert or semi-arid areas, when El Niño occurs.

The Ozone Layer

There is a hole in the ozone layer over Antarctica that is severely affecting the far southern portion of Chile. There have been rumors (not scientifically supported) of deformed livestock born in the south of Chile. As part of a tour, Susan was taken to a farm to see a five-legged cow!

Inversión Térmica

Inversión térmica (thermal inversion) is a phenomenon occurring in Santiago that affects the circulation of wind, causing surface air to become trapped. This is particularly harmful because it does not allow the pollution emitted by vehicles and factories to escape. Instead it hangs over the entire city like a big black cloud.

THE ECONOMY

Chile is often referred to as the star of Latin America in terms of its economic performance, and the government does much to encourage this image. In fact, Chileans have every right to be proud of the economy. In the wake of free-market reforms which promote foreign trade and privatization, Chile is one of the fastest growing economies in Latin America. GDP growth has been steady and impressive and the country currently enjoys a trade surplus. Inflation has been reduced to single-digit figures and the unemployment rate is relatively low. Moreover, military spending has dropped by more than half with the return of a civilian government.

The explosive growth of the Chilean economy is reflected in the dramatic increase of new construction.

19

Chile's geographical location has always contributed to the isolation of the country. This isolation has greatly affected the country's economy as well as other aspects of Chilean life. Prior to the late 1970s, the market had been closed. The country was dependent on one single export product – copper. The change over the past 20 years has been drastic. Chile now exports thousands of products, which are becoming well-known the world over. And on the flip side, Chileans now have access to a wider array of consumer goods. The country is more affluent than ever before. Yet, while in general Chileans are doing better, close to one-third of the population lives below the poverty line. Furthermore, the gap between the "haves" and the "have nots" is widening. In fact, it is one of the most severe in all of Latin America.

A Brief History

Like most Latin American countries during the 1940–60s, Chile practiced Import-Substitution Industrialization (ISI). The goal of ISI was to free the country from dependence on foreign economies through domestic or regional industrialization. Production took place within the country's borders and high tariffs and non-tariff barriers were erected to protect these struggling industries. Chilean products faced very little competition since imports were severely restricted. This led to inefficiency and high prices.

Socialism

The struggling economy came to a virtual standstill following the election of Salvador Allende, a socialist, in 1970. A combination of many factors, primarily bad policies and international and domestic sabotage, led to the ruin of the economy. Allende nationalized a great many industries and populist policies such as price controls led to shortages. This was aggravated by the increasing number of factories being taken over by workers, which reduced overall productivity. Inflation spiraled out of control and a black market emerged. A series of strikes and the cessation of international investment sealed its fate.

The Military Government and Free-Market Reforms

The military regime which ousted Allende in a coup in 1973 immediately focused on the economy. In the mid-1970s the Pinochet government, advised by a number of technocrats educated at the University of Chicago, known as the "Chicago Boys," implemented a process of rapid economic liberalization. Tariffs were reduced and non-tariff barriers were eliminated. This strategy was implemented to make domestic production more efficient as Chilean firms faced an influx of imports. The government also sought to diversify the economy, eliminating the country's dependence on copper. A series of privatizations were initiated and the role of the state was severely reduced. Part of the military dictatorship's policy included outlawing labor unions and repressing any form of dissent or protest. Workers were effectively and harshly prevented from bargaining or demonstrating to improve wages or working conditions, which had sunk very low. A number of Chilean firms went bankrupt in the face of stiff international competition, which led to further hardship when people lost their jobs. Unemployment increased dramatically and the number of Chileans living below the poverty line rose to over 40 percent. In 1983 the economy fell into a deep recession. It took over three years for the country to recover.

Many analysts credit the military government with saving the Chilean economy. However, it should not be overlooked that while the wealthy got wealthier, many Chileans sunk into poverty with no means of escaping. Furthermore, many observers continue to debate to this day whether these severe economic reforms could have been carried out under a democratic government.

Current Economy

By the time a democratic government was elected to power in 1990, the economy was strong. Democratic governments have continued with essentially the same economic policies instituted by the military regime. Today, there is a uniform tariff rate of 11 percent on all imported items and it will be reduced even further. Unlike the military government, however, democratic regimes have implemented a wide array of social policies and programs, and labor unions are no longer illegal. The number of Chileans living below the poverty line has fallen to about 30 percent.

Exports

The Chilean economy is export led. Chilean products are becoming well-known throughout the world for their high quality, especially Chilean wine, fruit, vegetables, paper and seafood. Roughly one-third of Chilean products are exported to Asia, one-third to the European Community and the other third throughout the Americas (slightly more than half to other Latin American countries and the remainder

A large percentage of Chilean exports pass through Valparaíso, the country's main port.

going to the US). In fact, one of Chile's main trading partners is Japan, with which it enjoys a trade surplus. Japan imports large amounts of Chilean copper and wood products. The United States alternates with Japan as Chile's main trading partner. Next in importance are the United Kingdom, Brazil, Germany and Argentina. This strategy of promoting exports across the globe lessens Chilean dependence on one trading partner.

Part of Chile's success can be attributed to the diversification of its exports. At one point, copper sales made up 80 percent of the country's exports. That figure has dropped by more than half. Chile has turned to the strengths of its widely differing regions and each makes a significant contribution to the Chilean economy. The north is the heart of the mining industry and the Central Valley is well-known for its agricultural produce. Forestry, fishing and tourism bring in dollars in the south. As a result, Chile now exports more than 3,400 distinct products. Some of the most important sectors of the economy are listed below.

Mining

Mining was and continues to be a fundamental component of the Chilean economy. Nitrate deposits in the northern regions were big business during the second half of the nineteenth century, so much so that it was called "white gold." At its height, there were over 60 mines in the Atacama Desert with 15,000 workers. However, synthetic nitrates invented by the Germans during World War I offered a cheap alternative and soon the desert was littered with abandoned mines. Fortunately, nitrate was not the only valuable mineral of the northern desert. Chile has the world's largest reserves of copper (around one-quarter of global supplies) and is the number one exporter of copper in the world. Chile has the second largest reserves of lithium and also has substantial reserves of iron, silver, salt, zinc, manganese, molyb-denum, gold, coal, iodine and has moderate reserves of oil and natural gas in the extreme south.

The CODELCO Case

The most infamous economic scandal in recent Chilean history is the CODELCO case. In 1993, Juan Pablo Dávila, a futures trader for CODELCO, the government copper corporation, lost over US$200 million in bad trades. Investigations have found that Dávila has some offshore accounts and it is believed that it was not bad bets, but rather a money-making scheme. The case is ongoing and to date only Dávila has been implicated.

Agriculture

Farming and agro-industries play a major role in the economy. Chile grows a wide variety of fruits and vegetables for export. Fresh and processed fruits and vegetables account for more than 70 percent of total agricultural exports. Chilean produce has a ready market during the winter season in the northern hemisphere. These products include grapes, apples, pears, kiwis, plums, nectarines, peaches, asparagus, tomatoes and corn. In fact, Chile is the world's largest exporter of grapes.

In 1989, an anonymous tip-off alerted US officials at the American Embassy in Santiago that grapes in a large shipment originating in Chile had been poisoned with cyanide. The US immediately suspended all imports of grapes, as did many other countries. The Chilean economy suffered greatly as a result. Citing procedural errors in the US government lab that had run the tests on the grapes, the Chilean government and private Chilean companies have demanded compensation from the US government. The case has never been resolved and continues to be an important issue in US–Chilean relations.

Wines

Chilean wines have also emerged prominently in the global market. They have a strong reputation as being good quality wines at affordable prices. Chile's distinct geography has proven useful to the wine industry. The sea to the west and the Andes Mountains to the east have protected the vines from foreign insects and diseases. In fact, the Andes protected Chilean vineyards from phylloxera, a disease that had severely damaged the wine industry in Europe.

Forestry

The forestry sector is vital to the Chilean economy. Forty-five percent of the land is suitable for forestry and 7.6 million hectares are covered by native forests. However, most of the industry uses plantations, which cover 1.6 million hectares. The majority of trees cultivated are Radiata pine and eucalyptus because they grow significantly faster in Chile than in other countries. Chile is among the world's largest

exporters of cellulose acetate. Chile's other principal wood exports are pulp, chips, sawn wood and paper.

Fishing

One of the most dynamic sectors of the Chilean economy has been the fishing industry. Due to the cold waters of the Pacific Ocean coming from Antarctica, Chile is an optimal place for a wide variety of fish and seafood. The development of salmon farms has been especially impressive. Chile began exporting salmon in 1984 and in only 10 years rose to be the second largest exporter of salmon in the world behind Norway. Other products include trout, hake, cod, kingclip, sea bass, swordfish, abalone, sea urchin, scallops, octopus, shrimp and crabs. Chile is also the largest exporter of fishmeal in the world.

Tourism

Due to its spectacular beauty and the abundance of volcanoes, mountains, rivers, fjords and glaciers, Chile attracts people from all over the world, especially those interested in adventure tourism. In total, revenue from tourism makes up nine percent of Chile's total foreign earnings.

Foreign Investment

Chile receives the highest level of foreign investment as a percentage of GDP in all of Latin America. Top investors are the United States, Canada, Finland, the United Kingdom, Japan and Australia. The main beneficiary of foreign capital is the mining sector. Other areas that receive significant amounts of foreign capital are infrastructure, energy, telecommunications and forestry. Local and foreign businesses may undertake a public works project as a concession, and recoup their investment through user fees collected during the length of the contract. This rise in foreign investment has been accompanied by a change in attitude. Foreign capital is now seen as a business partner in the country's development. This is a drastic change from the 1960s when the predominant view was that multinational corporations served only to strip the country of its wealth without stimulating further development.

Investment Abroad

Not only does Chile receive a great deal of foreign capital, but Chilean firms themselves are also investing abroad. Over half of all foreign investment has been made in Argentina. Chilean firms are also investing in Peru, Bolivia and Brazil. These investments are taking place in sectors such as banking, insurance, supermarkets, electricity distribution, telecommunications, computer software and the manufacturing of cookies and candy. Chile is also providing "technical exports," i.e., the transfer of knowledge and expertise. Chileans boast about the fact that their pension and health care systems are being studied carefully by several other countries. Chilean assistance has been provided in designing and setting up similar systems elsewhere.

Private Pension System

Chile implemented a reform of its pension fund system in the early 1980s. This successful program has been studied by many other countries in the region, even the United States. All new workers entering the labor force must choose a private, for-profit Pension Fund Administrator (AFP). Workers who were already in the labor force at the time of the reform had the option of choosing a private company or staying with the old system. Each employee has 10 percent of his or her salary deducted. This money goes into his or her personal retirement account which is not tied to his or her place of work. A percentage of the deduction covers service charges, disability and survivor's benefits. Anyone who wishes, may have a higher percentage deducted from his or her salary. Workers choose their AFP according to level of risk and/or rate of return. Because the fund managers are private, there is ample opportunity for competition. AFPs have been tightly regulated by the government, but these restrictions are starting to loosen. AFPs can now invest abroad and in a wider array of domestic sectors. Currently, retirees receive higher pensions compared to the old system and workers know the exact amount of their retirement funds at all times. The government guarantees a minimum pension in the event that AFP payouts fall below the subsistence level. It has also dramatically raised savings in Chile, which now boasts the highest savings rate in Latin America, one which is on par with developed countries. Criticisms of the new AFP system include high administrative fees, a "loss of solidarity" (because the new system emphasizes individual planning over large group funds), irregular practices to entice individuals to transfer to another AFP and cozy relations between the AFPs and the companies whose stock is being bought by the pension fund managers.

Regional Free Trade Agreements

Chile has signed a number of free trade agreements focusing on the three most important regions – the Americas, Asia and Europe. Chile has signed a free trade agreement with MERCOSUR, the South American Customs Union comprised of Argentina, Brazil, Paraguay and Uruguay. It has also signed separate free trade agreements with Colombia, Venezuela and Ecuador and hopes to conclude agreements with Peru and Bolivia shortly. Chile has finalized a free trade deal with Canada and has a free trade arrangement with Mexico. It also hopes to one day become a member of NAFTA, the North American Free Trade Agreement.

Chile is a member of APEC (Asia-Pacific Economic Cooperation) and PECC (Pacific Economic Cooperation Council). The APEC economies, which include Mexico, Peru, Canada, Russia and the US as well as Asian economies, represent Chile's most important markets. A framework agreement on trade with the European Community has also been reached.

— Chapter Two —

OVER FIVE HUNDRED YEARS OF HISTORY

PRE-COLUMBIAN HISTORY

When Pedro de Valdivia first arrived in what is now known as Chile, a number of native peoples inhabited this corner of the world. Sadly, the Spanish conquest, which brought war and slavery and introduced a number of fatal diseases, and the subsequent policies of the newly founded republic, caused many of the indigenous groups to disappear forever.

The Aymara were shepherds and farmers living in the Altiplano in northern Chile and are related to the Aymara of Bolivia. The Atacameños lived in the region between Arica and San Pedro de Atacama. The Diaguitas, well known for their pottery, lived in the valleys between Copiapó and just north of Santiago. The Picunche ("men of the north") inhabited the Central Valley bordered by the Aconcagua River, just north of Santiago, and the Bío Bío River to the south. All of these groups were brought under the control of the Incan empire in the mid-15th century. The Incan empire did not drastically alter their lifestyles – each group was only expected to pay tribute and provide labor when necessary. The garrisons were recalled to Cuzco (Peru) during an internal power struggle and Francisco Pizarro's arrival in Peru shortly thereafter brought an end to the Incan empire.

The native peoples of southern Chile were never successfully brought under Incan control. The Mapuche ("people of the land"), who lived south of the Bío Bío River, were the fiercest warriors. Not only were they successful in repelling the Incan warriors, but they also proved to be a formidable enemy of the Spanish. In fact, their resistance made Chile the most difficult country in the hemisphere to conquer. They taught themselves how to ride horses obtained from the Spanish and became expert cavalrymen.

The Huilliches ("men of the south") and the nomadic groups, the Pehuenches, Puelches and Tehuelches, lived further south. The Chonos inhabited the area known today as Aisén. The Alacaluf or Kawasqar were a nomadic tribe that moved along the channels to the far south in their canoes. The Aonikenk lived and roamed along the steppes of the southern Andes. The Selknam (Ona) lived in the northern parts of Tierra del Fuego and the Yamana (Yagan) lived along the southern coast near the Beagle Channel. Due to the severe cold, many of the indigenous peoples in southern Chile wore large pelts wrapped around their feet. The Spanish explorers referred to them as Patagones (big feet) and that is how the region became known as Patagonia. When Magellan sailed through the strait that now bears his name, he and his crew saw a great many bonfires used by the natives for warmth and cooking. They called the area Tierra del Fuego (land of fire), which is how such a cold region earned such a hot name.

THE CONQUISTADORS

After an unsuccessful expedition by Diego de Almagro, Pedro de Valdivia established a settlement on the Mapocho River on February 12, 1541, in the center of present-day Santiago. Within 20 years a number of other cities had been founded and Chile had become a General Captaincy under the Viceroyalty of Peru. However, due to the lack of valuable minerals such as silver and gold, and the country's remoteness, Chile remained a relatively unimportant part of Spain's colonial empire. Because wealth could only be earned through work such as farming and mining, there was no great migration to Chile. The colony's population never exceeded 500,000, the majority of whom were poor Spaniards. Chile grew into a rural economy and the upper classes were primarily landowners. However, due to climate and farming methods, slave labor was practically non-existent.

INDEPENDENCE

During the 18th century, a new class took form. The *criollos* were descendants of Spaniards born in Chile. They felt closer to their American land than to Europe and became the main force behind the movement that would give Chile its independence.

The struggle for autonomy began with the appointment of a Junta de Gobierno (Governing Council) on September 18, 1810. (Chileans celebrate this day as their National Day.) Napoleon's army had invaded Spain in 1808, deposed the king and placed Napoleon's brother on the throne. In Chile, as in other colonies, the governor called an open town meeting to elect a Junta de Gobierno that would govern in the name of the legitimate Spanish king. Although this *junta* pledged loyalty to the Spanish crown, it slowly pushed the country towards independence. Between 1811 and 1814 tension was high between royalists and separatists. Eventually, José Miguel Carrera seized power and refused to obey edicts from Spain.

In 1813 Spanish troops invaded Chile and took control of Talcahuano and Concepción before their march towards Santiago. Carrera took command of the army and worked closely with Bernardo O'Higgins to defend the capital. In October 1814 the Spanish defeated the Chilean army at the Battle of Rancagua. The separatists fled to Mendoza, Argentina.

Spanish rule was harsh. Supporters of independence were punished, movement was restricted and reforms were repealed. Spain's heavy hand convinced Chileans that the country needed independence. Meanwhile, O'Higgins had joined forces with José de San Martín, an Argentinean military leader. In 1817, they crossed the Andes into Chile and on February 12, 1818 defeated the Spanish at the Battle of Chacabuco.

THE NEW REPUBLIC

An open town meeting elected O'Higgins as supreme director and he ruled the country for five years. O'Higgins, who is today considered the liberator of Chile, was the illegitimate son of former governor Ambrosio O'Higgins, an Irishman, and a *criolla* woman from Chillán. He was popular with the people, but was not well-liked by the conservative aristocracy and was finally ousted in 1823.

There followed a relatively unstable period characterized by the struggle between conservatives (landowners and the church) and liberals (intellectuals who advocated the separation of church and state). In 1833 a new constitution was drafted and stood for almost 100 years. Created by the conservatives who had gained power, it established a strong central government and severely limited the powers of Congress. A strong presidency has persevered throughout Chilean history. Conservatives ruled Chile for a long period and the country settled into relative stability.

La Moneda, the presidential palace, is a long-standing symbol of democracy.

THE WAR OF THE PACIFIC

The War of the Pacific was waged from 1879 until 1883 and pitted Chile against a united Peru and Bolivia for control of the Atacama Desert. All three countries claimed parts of the desert. In fact, prior to the war Bolivia had extended all the way to the coast at Antofagasta, and Arica belonged to Peru. This area contained huge mineral deposits, especially sodium nitrate. Chileans began mining in parts of Peru and Bolivia, for which they paid royalties to both governments. However, the two countries became fearful of Chilean expansion and formed a secret alliance. Between 1875 and 1878 Peru and Bolivia seized all Chilean claims, a move which led to war in February 1879. Chile, home of the best navy in the Pacific, ultimately defeated Peru and Bolivia in 1883 and took possession of Arica, Tacna and Antofagasta. Tacna was returned to Peru 10 years later.

CIVIL WAR

In 1886 the liberal president José Manuel Balmaceda made attempts to increase government involvement in the economy and started a number of public works. The demand for higher taxes, however, was staunchly opposed by Congress, which represented the interests of the oligarchy. Political instability ensued. The mining region in the north became a rebel stronghold led by mine owners unwilling to pay higher nitrate taxes. Finally, with the backing of the navy, the rebels met Balmaceda's army at Concón and La Placilla in 1891 and civil war erupted. It was the bloodiest period in Chilean history, with over 10,000 victims in only eight months of fighting. Balmaceda's forces were defeated. He sought refuge in the Argentine embassy where he later committed suicide. The war resulted in increased congressional power and a "semi-parliamentary" system.

POPULISM

Despite the power of the oligarchy, workers and the newly emerging middle class wielded a small degree of influence. In 1920, Chile's first populist president, Arturo Alessandri, was elected. He met with strong opposition from Congress and in 1925, when the two branches of government had reached an impasse, the military intervened and installed Carlos Ibáñez as president. A new constitution was written, which reinforced the power of the presidency.

Chileans were shocked by the military intervention. Although the country's former governments had been less than fully democratic, Chile had not been subject to recurrent military coups as had other Latin American countries. When the worldwide depression hit in 1929, Chile experienced a severe economic crisis and the military president was forced to step down in disgrace.

THE SOCIALIST REPUBLIC

The year following the military leader's ouster was characterized by instability. During this period, Colonel Marmaduque Grove installed a "Socialist Republic." Although it lasted for a very short time, it is an important moment in Chile's history as it paved the way for the formation of the Socialist Party the following year.

THE POPULAR FRONT

At the end of this tumultuous year, Arturo Alessandri was once again elected president. Now ruling with full authority, Alessandri planned and executed the country's economic recovery. However, it was not without repression, particularly of workers and the left. More unified in their opposition to Alessandri than in their ideological beliefs, the parties of the left and center formed an alliance called the Frente Popular (Popular Front).

By the presidential election of 1938, the Popular Front had become a coalition of several parties, including the Radicals, Socialists, Communists, Democrats and Confederation of Chilean Workers. Their candidate, Pedro Aguirre Cerda, narrowly defeated the right-wing candidate to become president in 1938. Aguirre represented businessmen and the growing middle class, which began to play an active role in government for the first time.

Aguirre faced opposition both from the right, which controlled Congress, and from within the coalition. He was forced to leave office in 1941 due to poor health and the Popular Front was soon dismantled.

A POLARIZED SOCIETY

With the demise of the Popular Front, the Chilean political system underwent major changes. The large number of political parties led to fierce competition and coalition-building. Alliances were fragile, and Chilean society became increasingly polarized between the right, center and left.

The 1952 presidential election was the first of a series with no majority vote. Candidates took office with less than 50 percent of the vote. The fragmentation of the electorate continued and in 1958 Jorge Alessandri, son of Arturo Alessandri, the candidate for the right, took office with only 31.6 percent of the vote. The second runner-up, Salvador Allende, the candidate of the Socialist-Communist Alliance (FRAP), finished only 2.5 percentage points behind Alessandri.

CHRISTIAN DEMOCRATS

Jorge Alessandri was unable to resolve the severe socio-economic problems plaguing the country. This led many Chileans to the conclusion that the parties of the right did not have the answers. A new party, the Christian Democrats, had emerged in the late 1950s. Its goal was to make Chile a more just and equitable society through reform. While the right was not comfortable with these reformist ideas, it feared a possible victory by the left, and therefore pledged its support to the Christian Democrat candidate, Eduardo Frei Montalva. It is important to note that while Frei won the 1964 presidential election with 56 percent of the vote, Allende received 39 percent.

Many Chileans speak of Frei with great respect. During his term, land reforms and the nationalization of the copper industry were

The legislative branch, formerly housed in this building, reflected the deep division between Chile's main political forces.

initiated. The middle and lower classes were invited to participate in government. However, Frei was prohibited by law from running for another term, and the right, which never really backed the Christian Democrats' platform, withdrew their support and ran their own candidate, Jorge Alessandri, in the next presidential election in 1970. The left again chose Salvador Allende, a Socialist Senator. Allende

37

won a plurality with 36.3 percent of the vote. Ironically, he won the presidency with fewer votes than he had garnered in the 1964 election.

SALVADOR ALLENDE

Allende's victory marked the first time in history that a Marxist had been legally and democratically elected president of any country. He pledged a "transition to socialism" within the limits of the law. Allende completed the nationalization of the copper industry, which until then had been controlled primarily by American firms. While most Chileans supported this move, there was growing unrest as the coal, steel and banking industries were targeted for nationalization. Private factories were taken over by workers or by state appointed "overseers" which led to a decline in overall production. As goods disappeared from store shelves, Chileans were forced to make purchases on the black market. Anger and resentment brewed among both the upper and middle classes and the international community. The US called for an end to aid and credit. Without the support of international agencies and the lack of private foreign investment, things looked bleak.

It is important to understand the mood that existed in Chile prior to the 1973 coup. Economic and political problems affected a broad section of Chilean society. Workers benefited from some of Allende's policies – initially they were enjoying higher wages and subsidized food prices and actively participated in the community and workplace. Yet, many Chileans opposed the Socialist regime and feared the consequences of the political, social and economic disarray into which the country had fallen. By 1972, acts of violence, protests and strikes were regular throughout Chile.

Escalating Violence

As 1973 progressed, confrontation increased. More and more Chileans believed there was no peaceful solution and feared that severe violence would erupt well before the next election in 1976.

Rumors of a coup had been spreading for quite awhile when Allende received news that the navy had stormed Valparaíso on the morning of September 11, 1973. Allende was offered safe passage and exile, but he adamantly refused. Instead he left his home and went to La Moneda, the presidential palace in the center of Santiago. He took up arms to defend himself and his vision for Chile. Later that morning he made a moving speech broadcast on the radio, describing his hopes and plans for the country he loved, and denouncing those he considered traitors. He proclaimed that the "free man" would ultimately prevail. The Ministry of Defense faced La Moneda from across the Alameda (the main thoroughfare) and throughout the morning troops exchanged fire with Allende's supporters. The bullet holes remain to this day in the walls of the Ministry of Defense.

Close to noon, air force jets bombed La Moneda, destroying a long-standing symbol of democratic government. Allende's last moments are unclear; whether he committed suicide or was killed by army troops remains a mystery. But what is clear is that the socialist experiment in Chile had come to a violent end.

While it is well-known that the CIA was involved in the coup, its role is sometimes overstated. It is true that the US attempted to sabotage the Allende government from the beginning and backed the coup, but the Chilean political system had disintegrated of its own accord. If you enter into a conversation with a Chilean and boldly assert that the US government was to blame, not only will you show your ignorance of the facts and lack of understanding of the situation prior to the coup, but you will also be arrogantly overstating the power and influence of the US on Chilean politics. Pinochet was in no way a puppet of the US. Allende's memory is preserved today with great respect and admiration by his supporters on the left and by many around the world who see him as a political hero who died for his ideals. For many others, however, Allende will always be associated with chaos and disruption.

GENERAL AUGUSTO PINOCHET

Following the coup, a military *junta* led by General Augusto Pinochet immediately seized control of the government. The *junta* was comprised of the commanders-in-chief of the four armed forces, the army, navy, air force and Carabineros (uniformed national police). Many who had ties with the communist and socialist parties were rounded up and detained. Most were painfully tortured to extract information on other members or activists. Some detainees were released, some imprisoned and many forced into exile. Others were executed or simply disappeared. To the victims' family members, this is the worst of all possible situations. Figures vary depending upon the source, but estimates range from 2,000 to 6,000 people "disappeared" during the dictatorship.

The *junta* dissolved Congress, suspended the constitution, declared all political parties illegal and disbanded labor unions. In order to maintain tight control, the junta restricted the media, imposed a 9 p.m. curfew and took over the universities. A secret and highly feared police force was in charge of silencing dissent.

For those suspected of having supported the Allende government life became a nightmare, but for others the coup represented a return to stability. Food and other items were once again available in stores. Many who initially supported the coup believed that power would soon be handed back to the civilian government. As time passed, however, and General Pinochet consolidated his power, it became apparent that he was there to stay. In January 1974, Pinochet announced that the military regime would remain in power for no less than five years.

THE CHICAGO BOYS

After having "secured" the country by ridding it of the communists and socialists, the military immediately turned to the economy. A number of civilian technocrats who had been educated at the Univer-

sity of Chicago proposed radical adjustments in economic policy. The "Chicago Boys," as they were known, promoted a free market economy and a drastic reduction in the role of the state. These policies were effective in reducing inflation from about 500 percent at the time of the coup to 10 percent in 1982. The country began to enjoy economic growth and had ended its unhealthy dependence on copper.

However, there were problems. Lower tariffs and the removal of import quotas forced inefficient Chilean industries to compete with international firms. As a result, many were forced out of business which led to high levels of unemployment among the working class. By 1983 unemployment had reached 33 percent and the country suffered from the highest per capita foreign debt in the world. The populace protested and a great many demonstrations were held in Santiago and other cities, in spite of harsh government reprisals. Although political parties were still illegal, de facto opposition parties still existed and were the force behind the one-day strikes. The protests, however, did not achieve the ultimate goal of ousting the government.

THE "NO" CAMPAIGN

A plebiscite held in 1980 had ratified a new constitution that secured Pinochet's presidency until 1990. By the mid-1980s it became apparent that Pinochet wanted to extend his term in office within a constitutional framework. Another plebiscite was called in October 1988 which would determine whether he would continue as president of Chile until 1998. A massive "No" campaign was undertaken that would ultimately deny Pinochet another presidential term. Although the "No" campaign received substantial aid from international agencies in terms of both organization and financing, it was a Chilean movement. By this time, self-exiles had begun to return in order to help precipitate Pinochet's end. To say that foreign powers brought the end of the military regime would grossly overemphasize their role.

A NARROW DEFEAT

Pinochet stepped down in 1990 after negotiations with the incoming democratic government. According to some accounts, he ultimately disregarded the advice of some of his closest advisors who recommended that he keep ruling by force. It is very important to remember that although he lost, Pinochet received 40 percent of the vote. That means that after 16 years in power, a substantial share of the population still supported his policies. We have found, in talking with people from democratic countries, that there is an overwhelming assumption that all Chileans were against Pinochet. How could anyone support a dictatorship that systematically violated human rights? Yet, if one fully understands the situation before the coup – severe economic problems and fear of communist take-over – it begins to make some sense. The Pinochet government had played upon these old fears and focused on the flourishing economy during its campaign.

THE CONCERTACIÓN

Following the victory of the "No" campaign, a presidential election was called for December 1989 to choose a transitional government. The Christian Democrats joined with the "democratic left" – the Socialist Party and the Party for Democracy (PPD) and a number of fringe parties – to form the Concertación. Although political parties had been outlawed during the military regime, the large parties were never fully disbanded. The Concertación chose Patricio Aylwin, a Christian Democrat, as its candidate. A lawyer and college professor, Aylwin was a former member of Congress and party leader. The right-wing candidate was Hernán Büchi, Finance Minister during the Pinochet government. Aylwin won a clear victory and assumed the presidency for a four-year term.

AYLWIN'S PRESIDENCY

A gentle man held in high esteem, Aylwin seemed to be the best choice for a transition. The president who was to lead Chile to democracy needed to be a widely respected man with high moral standing. Aylwin successfully walked a fine line in dealing with the most important issue of his presidency – human rights – while not offending or alienating the military. His administration needed to maintain a strong economic performance while boosting social expenditure. With the return of democracy, many new voices were clamoring to be heard. Aylwin was able to find channels for these groups to express themselves without straining the fledgling system.

Pinochet continued as Commander-in-Chief of the Army until his term ended in 1998. Although he held considerable influence and was often in the news, he did not control the government. The 1980 constitution called for the inclusion of nine designated senators, who are not elected, but were named by the outgoing Pinochet government. These appointed senators have prevented the Concertación from gaining a majority in the upper house. In 1998 Pinochet became an appointed senator of the same Congress he shut down. This has become a highly sensitive political and moral issue in Chile.

HUMAN RIGHTS

When Pinochet stepped down from the presidency, he vowed that he would not allow even one of his soldiers to be tried for human rights violations. With the exception of a few very important cases, this has been the case in Chile. Some of the most publicized and shocking human rights cases include El Caso de Los Quemados (two young demonstrators who were burned alive, one of whom – Carmen Gloria Quintana – survived), Los Degollados (four activists who were found

CUT, the national labor union, peacefully protests outside its main headquarters, a sign that it is slowly recovering from the many years of repression under military rule.

with their throats slashed), El Caso Soria (a Spanish national who worked for the United Nations and was summarily executed), the assassination of Orlando Letelier, the former Chilean Ambassador to the United States under the Allende government, and his American assistant in Washington D.C. and the assassination of former Commander-in-Chief of the Army General Carlos Prats and his wife in Buenos Aires. Under President Aylwin a "Truth and Reconciliation Commission" was established to investigate human rights violations and, wherever possible, bring the accused to trial. It was non-confrontational and served to defuse the issue, but many argue that it did not go far enough. Recently, a new approach is being used by the families of human rights victims. They are filing civil lawsuits, arguing that the human rights abuses were committed by agents of the state. According to the Rettig Report (the document issued by the reconciliation commission), there are over 1,000 documented cases where violations were committed by state agents, making them eligible for this type of lawsuit. Whether this is better than an open and confrontational investigation, as in South Africa, can only be determined with time.

EDUARDO FREI RUIZ-TAGLE

In 1993, the Concertación candidate, Eduardo Frei Ruiz-Tagle, a Christian Democrat and the son of Eduardo Frei Montalva, was elected president by a wide margin.

Analysts are concerned about the durability of the Concertación, where the Socialist Party and the PPD have taken a back-seat to the Christian Democrats. Questions abound regarding how long the Socialists, a political force that has worked hard to rebuild and reshape itself, will be content in the number two position.

Chapter Three

CARMEN MIRANDA WAS NOT CHILEAN!

A HOMOGENEOUS SOCIETY

The first thing you may notice about Chilean society is that it is very homogeneous. In spite of the presence of minority groups, they do not stand out and demand attention. They have either immersed themselves in the dominant culture or have maintained their differences while remaining on the edge of mainstream society. Chileans generally regard themselves as one people.

ETHNICITY

Upon arriving in Chile, most people are struck by the fact that the population seems so "European." In contrast to their northern neighbors Peru and Bolivia, Chileans have a high percentage of European blood. The majority of Chileans could very well be classified as *mestizo*. Although Chileans do have Mapuche blood, many do not consider it part of their cultural identity since they do not speak the language or participate in Mapuche traditions. Many Chileans may not be aware of their entire family background. Often the lack of knowledge is part of a cultural amnesia that is common in Latin America. The Spanish must accept some of the blame: there is a long tradition in Spain of "purity of blood" that resulted in the persecution of minority groups. This attitude traveled to the Americas even though few Spanish women were brought to the New World. Most of the early Spanish settlers kept Indian concubines. A friend once said, "If you shake the family tree, an Indian woman is likely to fall out." However, the general mindset effectively rejects this historical truth and instead identifies with a more Chilean–European self-concept. Do not presume that Chilean friends, no matter how dark their skin, consider themselves to be part Mapuche or any other Amerindian group.

This sculpture in Santiago's main square honors Chile's indigenous ancestry.

Mapuche

The Mapuche are considered a distinct group with their own set of customs and traditions. Although Chileans are proud of the fierce and powerful Mapuche warrior legacy, Indians, in general, tend to be looked down upon and the term *indio* possesses negative connotations (lazy, stubborn). They are at the low end of the social stratum, due in large part to high levels of poverty.

The Pre-Columbian Museum in Santiago boasts a spectacular collection of indigenous artifacts. Mapuche crafts can be found at craft fairs, but unless you travel to the Temuco area, there is a striking absence of Mapuche culture in everyday Chilean society.

The German Community

One large minority group which has retained much of its culture is the Germans. A government program implemented between 1852 and 1880 encouraged the mass immigration of Germans to tame the south. Most German families remain in the Lake District, especially in the cities of Puerto Montt, Puerto Varas, Osorno, Valdivia and Temuco. German is still spoken by members of the community and some speak Spanish with an accent. They tend to marry amongst themselves. If you do travel to the south, you must eat in a Club Alemán (German Club). They are found in every city throughout the south. Excellent German meals are served and it is interesting to watch the men gather to socialize and play cards. Also, *once* (afternoon tea) is a real treat here served with German delicacies such as *kuchen* and *strudel*.

Colonia Dignidad

No doubt you will hear talk of Colonia Dignidad (Dignity Colony) and if you remain unclear as to just exactly what it is, you are not alone. Rumors abound and many stories are passed around, but it is difficult to confirm much of anything. What is known is that Colonia Dignidad is a cult-like, isolationist German group that lives on a well-protected farm near Chillán in southern Chile. The colony was established in the

1960s and no outsider has been able to determine exactly what goes on inside. During the dictatorship, it is believed that it aided the military in dealing with opposition. Allegations against the group include child abuse, torture and kidnapping. The current democratic government, the Chilean judiciary and the German government have taken a strong position against the colony's leaders.

Despite public concerns, the colony has some vocal supporters, particularly in the area where it is located. Colonia Dignidad runs a small hospital that provides health care to the local populace and also runs a very good German restaurant that is open to the public.

Other Groups

A number of other ethnic groups have also immigrated and subsequently integrated into Chilean culture. Croatian immigrants went to Punta Arenas and have slowly migrated north. You will notice that a significant number of Chileans have surnames that end with the trademark "ic."

The British also came to Chile during the late 1800s, primarily as advisors to the newly established Chilean navy and as merchants. In addition to their influence on the navy, they are credited with the introduction of afternoon tea in Chile.

A number of influential families in Chile are of British descent. The Edwards family is the most prominent (they own Chile's main daily, *El Mercurio*, and founded Banco Edwards, a major bank).

Other ethnic groups like the Italians and the French came in smaller numbers. The Welsh traveled to Patagonia to herd sheep and have remained, for the most part, isolated in that desolate part of the continent. Jews also came to Chile, by way of Argentina. Even though they have been influential in business, academia, the sciences and the arts, in general, the community has remained invisible. A student on a study abroad program said that her host family was shocked when she told them halfway through the year that she was Jewish. The family didn't know any Jews and assumed they were all Orthodox.

There are a few groups of gypsies in Chile. They generally live in segregated areas and are often the subject of discrimination and contempt.

As the Chilean economy grows, Latin Americans from poorer neighboring countries are increasingly immigrating (both legally and illegally) in search of work.

Unlike other Latin American countries, Chile did not import a significant number of slaves. The Chilean economy, although basically a rural economy, did not depend upon crops that required slave labor. Therefore, there are few blacks in Chile. As a result Chileans, in general, display great interest in blacks without treating them with hostility. An African-American woman in Chile on a study abroad program remarked that she was stared at quite a bit, but in general, treated very nicely.

Recently, Koreans, Taiwanese and other Asians have emigrated to Chile in significant numbers. Unlike other groups, due to their distinctive physical characteristics and radically different culture, Asians have not assimilated as easily. They are readily recognized as being different and have remained on the margins of mainstream society. With their arrival, Chileans have had to begin to learn how to accept those who "do not look like them."

DISCRIMINATION

Most Chileans will tell you that they are not racist, but because of their prior long-standing cultural isolation, this assertion has never really been put to the test. Chileans seem to make conflicting, sometimes shocking, statements without realizing the obvious contradictions. You'll often hear, "I'm not racist, but..." A Korean woman was expelled from a health club because, according to the management and other members, she smelled bad. The woman sued the health club, citing discrimination, and won the case. The first racial conflict the country has experienced in modern times occurred a few years ago when Korean youth gangs clashed with Chilean gangs. Authorities cracked down on the Korean gangs, threatening their whole families with expulsion if the criminal behavior continued. The issue was eventually resolved, but not before a number of Korean families were expelled.

Physically, Chileans resemble one another and look, for the most part, like one people. A very important consequence of this fact is that if you are not from Latin America, you will immediately be recognized as a foreigner. Despite the fact that Chile is opening to increasing numbers of foreigners, you will still attract attention and interest. Susan, a blonde, found that she was constantly stared at. Although it was annoying, it was neither hostile nor meant as a sexual advance. Once she knew it wasn't menacing, she learned to become oblivious to the stares.

CLASS STRUCTURE

The sharpest distinctions between Chileans lie in classes. Chilean society, in the past, was highly stratified according to income. Some families enjoyed vast wealth and power, and while most of these families have retained their fortunes, increased social mobility has brought some changes to Chilean society.

Old Money

Chile's early economy was based primarily on agriculture and mining and therefore the upper class consisted mainly of landowners. Today, the wealth remains in the hands of these same families. Early on, you will notice that the same surnames keep popping up in association with business, politics, etc. These are members of extended families and these familial ties are very important. Upon meeting someone, a Chilean can form an immediate, if not always correct, opinion based upon their surname. Some of the most recognizable families are Edwards, Matta, Lyon, Santa María, Matte, Aguirre, Undurraga, Errázuriz, and Larraín. Surnames with a double "r," such as the final four names, are Basque names and Chileans refer to them as *apellidos vinosos* (the wine surnames) because, among other things, these families owned the vineyards.

In Spanish-speaking cultures, each person has two surnames (*apellidos*), the first being that of the father and the second that of the mother (who does not change her name when she marries). This allows the public to know both families from which the person hails. For convenience, people may sometimes use only their first surname, but both are legal and are used in all formal occasions. Some Chileans that we met had trouble understanding why we only had one last name. They couldn't believe that the mother's name could be so easily discarded.

Yuppies

While the "old money" has maintained its status, a new group – yuppies – has emerged. As barriers to social mobility are broken down, the children of middle-class (and sometimes even lower-class) families have moved to the top of their fields and are enjoying the accompanying wealth. Yuppies, in general, are earning money in the "new" professions, primarily in the financial sector as brokers and consultants. A number are also industrialists and business leaders.

The wealth enjoyed by a greater percentage of the population has been accompanied by a growing exclusivity. In the past, established families were the only ones who enjoyed the finer things. Now, more people have access to these same things. In an effort to maintain a feeling of exclusivity, there has been a surge in the number of organizations that restrict access to the general public, for instance, private condominiums, clubs, etc. There are a few restaurants and bars that try to restrict entrance based on money or beauty, although this policy, condemned by the public, the media and the authorities is never stated outright.

The wealthy in Chile lead very comfortable lives, but Chileans in general tend not to be ostentatious. In fact, the president, once elected, continues to live in his home. Yet, this is slowly changing as those

Elegant houses located in the sprawling suburbs at the base of the mountains in Santiago reflect the country's newly acquired wealth and sophistication.

with newly acquired wealth feel the need to show off. Many of the affluent, both old and new money, live in large, secure homes at the base of the *cordillera* in Santiago, or other posh neighborhoods in various cities. Ironically, the affluent neighborhoods of Santiago are prone to high levels of pollution, and power and water shortages because of their location. Those who live in Santiago almost certainly have a beach house where they spend weekends.

Most also travel outside Chile, visiting the US and Europe. The latest trend is to visit the Asia-Pacific region. They also receive the best education and health care. Most attend private schools or one of the few prestigious public schools. They will either go to one of the two prominent universities (Universidad de Chile or La Universidad Católica) or will attend universities in the US or Europe. The most respected hospitals are located in the wealthier neighborhoods, and if special care is required, some may travel abroad. The main difference between old and new money, however, is the contacts the established families can call upon for favors. Old money relies on the "boys' clubs," networks of school friends and family to which the new money does not always have access.

The Middle Class

Chile has a large and stable middle class, accounting for nearly 40 percent of the population. Many Chileans classify themselves as middle class, even if they are in the lower income bracket. Bureaucrats, mid-level managers, professionals, office workers, teachers and nurses make up the bulk of the middle class.

The Lower Class

For all the accolades praising Chile as an economic miracle, the sad fact remains that over 30 percent of Chileans live below the internationally recognized poverty line. If you've never been to a developing country, you may be shocked by the amount of poverty you see. A European who was in Latin America for the first time drove past a *población* (poor neighborhood) and asked if human beings lived there. However, if you are familiar with Third World countries, Chile ranks among the best in addressing poverty.

Social Policies for Low-Income Sectors

Until recently, Chile has been applauded for its housing program. Prior to the 1970s, low-income groups built shanty towns using cardboard and metal on illegally seized land. Pinochet initiated a housing policy that relocated these groups to state supported housing. By removing the shanty town eyesores, he hoped to change foreign perceptions and attract capital. These housing policies were expanded and reinforced by the subsequent democratic governments.

There have been a number of criticisms leveled at the housing program. First, the houses are very small which leads to overcrowding, especially when extended family members share the same roof.

In Chile a relative will always be taken in until he can get back on his feet. Second, the people were relocated to cheap land on the periphery of the city. Third, the low quality of the construction materials became terribly evident following heavy rains, when many homes were damaged. Despite these drawbacks, residents have legal title to their property and access to electricity and running water. A very important side effect has been the sharp rise in health indexes. Infant mortality, maternal mortality and malnutrition levels are now almost on par with developed countries.

Although Chile has a very high literacy rate, the quality of education provided by public schools is well below that offered by private schools. The result is a large sector of the population with few skills who wind up either unemployed or underemployed. Recently, the government initiated extensive educational reforms designed to bridge the gap between public and private education.

Public health facilities are also substandard, and with the introduction of private health care (ISAPRES), many have opted to leave the public health care system altogether. One consequence is that less money is now being contributed to the public health care system (FONASA). Many doctors work in both private hospitals and public clinics. However, they are hampered by the run-down facilities and the inadequate equipment and supplies available in the public clinics. As a result, the level of care that the poor receive is overwhelmingly inferior to that received by the middle and upper classes.

The working poor rely heavily on public transportation, often taking long, crowded, uncomfortable bus rides to get to and from work. Since the *poblaciones* are located along the edge of Santiago, many are stuck for over $1^1/2$ hours in a bus just going one way. This should improve as metro service is expanded. When the heavy rains hit Santiago during the winter months, the poor neighborhoods are subject to floods that halt transportation and damage homes.

Drug abuse among teenagers and young adults in the *poblaciones* is a growing problem. The most common illicit drugs in Chile are marijuana and pasta base, a crude form of cocaine. Sniffing glue is another problem.

The harsh economic policies enforced during the military dictatorship caused a noticeable increase in the number of poor to well over 40 percent. Subsequent democratic governments have implemented programs and policies to reverse that trend with encouraging results. The percentage of indigent poor has dropped from almost 17 percent to nine percent. However, the gap between the "haves" and the "have nots" is large and growing. The highest concentration of poor live in the VIII Region, near Concepción. Many men from this region were coal miners before the mines were closed. The government hopes to alleviate the problem by providing retraining programs.

Exiliados and Retornados

Another sector of Chilean society worth mentioning is the *retornados*, exiles during the Pinochet regime who have since returned to Chile. This group has experienced a number of unique problems such as reintegration into a "foreign" culture and society. Some exiles who harbor old ideas are confronted with a new Chile, while others had grown accustomed to the culture of their host country. The children and foreign spouses of exiles also have problems living in a country they have never known and with which they feel no close bond.

Social Mobility

Increased social mobility has accompanied economic growth but it is probably not happening as rapidly as many would like. Chileans with a name and money definitely continue to have an advantage over others. Family members and friends (*pitutos*) are still called upon for favors and average work is quickly rewarded. Those without the benefit of a "good" surname or the appropriate credentials must work twice as hard to move ahead and are often promoted at a slower pace, but it is possible to advance.

While middle-class Chileans may complain about the way things work and how impossible it is to get ahead without *pitutos*, they must look to themselves as well for continuing the practice. Take a quick look at the names of politicians and you'll find the same names that have been in politics for generations. While family connections no doubt help a politician rise through the ranks, once his or her name is on the ballot, it is the average Chilean who votes them into office over an "unknown." This is not to say that these people are not capable, many serve their constituents well, but rather to point out that name recognition makes life in Chile much easier because of the widespread assumption that a member of a successful family will naturally excel.

Although some may complain about the power and wealth of the elite, the average Chilean would much rather join that sector than see it destroyed. The wealthy have maintained their place at the top of the social ladder and remain highly visible. The society pages, which in many modern cities have been relegated to the back pages, are one of the first things you see in *El Mercurio*, Santiago's most respected newspaper.

THE SOCIAL AGENDA

Issues traditionally at the forefront of debate, such as politics, economics and human rights, now compete with a wide array of topics that up until a few years ago were never discussed publicly. These include divorce, the environment, AIDS, abortion, sexuality, drugs, child abuse, etc. This radical opening comes in spite of the influence of conservative sectors of society, such as the Catholic Church.

While discussion of these issues is becoming more prevalent, the issues themselves are not necessarily being embraced. Societal attitudes towards homosexuals are stuck in the past, especially among people over 30. With the exception of artists, gays remain very much in the closet. The non-judgmental term, *homosexual*, is almost never used by Chileans, who seem to prefer the derogatory *maricón* or *fleto*.

A new class – yuppies – has emerged in Chile within the past 15 years or so.

Among the younger generations there may be less outright condemnation, but there are whispers and pointing.

The new social agenda reflects changes in societal values. Young people are breaking with the conservative attitudes of the past and as the country becomes a more active member of the global community, they are increasingly receptive to new and different ideas. Some may be viewed as refreshing and positive, while others may have negative implications. For example, money and the conspicuous consumption that it brings have made an impact on society. Chileans are much more competitive than in the past, always in hot pursuit of finalizing the deal and making a profit. Older Chileans are amazed at the amount of wealth and the monthly salaries of the younger generation. The country seems to be functioning at a new and higher energy level. You'll see quite a few cellular phones on the street and Chile now boasts the highest number of personal computers per capita in Latin America. The pressure to succeed can be seen in several spheres of life. A large percentage of drivers stopped by police for talking on the telephone while driving were actually using fake phones to keep up pretences. Another effect has been a certain arrogance towards Latin American neighbors. Some firms have ordered sensitivity classes for their employees to prevent the emergence of the "Ugly Chilean."

MYTHS

Curiously, one way in which Chileans express their pride to foreigners is to downplay their performance and insult themselves. Chileans ceaselessly complain that they are lazy, disorganized procrastinators. Even though there may be some truth to what they say, in reality the country functions extremely well. Given that it is the best-performing economy in Latin America, how could these self-recriminations be entirely true? This, of course, is one of the myths associated with Latin America that does not apply to Chile. Do not expect to encounter the stereotypical Latin American "fat cat," sitting behind his desk, wasting time. Chile runs well because of hard work, education and efficiency.

CONSUMER RIGHTS

As Chileans earn more money and increase consumption, they are slowly starting to demand rights as consumers. However, this is only a recent phenomenon. Most Chileans readily admit that they should demand better service and higher quality products, but then argue that they are just too lazy to follow it up. The government is helping to change this attitude. A Consumer Rights Law was recently passed and a new government agency was established to investigate complaints. Enforcement of the law is still weak and many Chileans do not fully understand their rights. Newspapers have also devoted a section to running stories of negligent businesses. However, if you are used to being on the receiving end of "the customer is always right" policy, you may be aggravated by the lack of anything comparable in Chile. Our advice is to be very sure of any purchase you make, because chances are you will be unable to return it. Exchanges are more common nowadays, but may require determination.

PERSONAL SPACE

Every society has its own definition of personal space. Americans generally keep a relatively large distance from others. Chileans tend to keep much less personal space. Do not be surprised to find the person behind you in line breathing down your neck and inadvertently poking you in the back. It is aggravating, but unfortunately there is nothing you can do to widen that space. You'll also notice that while most Chileans respect lines, a number of people will cut. They do so mainly because they can get away with it. This behavior is grudgingly accepted by those in line, who may grumble but would never confront the person outright.

A SOMBER PEOPLE

If you've never visited Latin America, the thought of going to Chile must conjure up a whole range of images. A recent survey conducted in the United States found that the number one image people associate with Chile is the Mexican *sombrero*. This demonstrates a very important point: Latin America is not one big country or culture. Differences abound within the region and Chileans, like others from the Southern Cone region, are the polar opposite of Latinos from the "tropical Caribbean" area. If this was your expectation you may be disappointed to find the mood in Chile very somber. You will not find scantily clad women with fruit on their heads! Chileans are not flashy and to be so is a sign of bad taste. They dress conservatively, and are very reserved when conducting business. Even their fiestas are restrained. Of course, some groups, such as artists and intellectuals, are the exception to the rule. In general, to be serious and somber is considered a positive attribute in Chile, especially in business. The best advice to the visitor is to keep it simple, don't dress in loud colors, get drunk or engage in rowdy behavior at a party.

CORRUPTION AND DRUG TRAFFICKING

Latin America also invokes images of rampant corruption and drug trafficking. While it would be incorrect to state that corruption is nonexistent in Chile (is there any country that can make that claim?), stiff penalties have kept the number of incidents relatively low. Offering or accepting a bribe is considered a serious offense and is not tolerated.

Furthermore, Chile is not a major player in the international drug trade. It is true that drug use is a problem in certain areas, but the business of drug trafficking has sidestepped Chile. Drugs are not grown or manufactured in Chile and while some drug traffickers would like to launder drug money through Chilean organizations, the government is cognizant of such efforts and the police work vigorously to thwart such activities. Any persons found having links with drug traffickers are punished accordingly.

A LEGALISTIC SOCIETY

The minute you arrive in Chile and begin the process of legalizing your stay, you will become painfully aware that this is a very legalistic society. Chilean society has been built on a number of laws, each of which carries considerable weight. This is made very clear the first time you stroll through the downtown streets. What at first glance looks like a newspaper and magazine kiosk is actually a kiosk selling complete copies of existing legislation. When a new law is passed, these booklets are hawked like any other prized commodity. This has led to a high degree of legal formality among Chileans. No matter what brings you to Chile, work or study, you will have to perform a series of *trámites* (legal transactions). Applications and documents

must be approved by various offices. It requires time and patience. Fortunately, the government is studying ways to make the entire process easier. Most likely any document you need to submit anywhere will first require notarization. Take a short walk through Santiago and you can't help but notice the abundance of notaries. Notaries are kept in business by the general attitude that a document is not valid if it has not been notarized. We had photocopies of our passports notarized and carried those with us instead of the real document in case of theft or loss. To a Chilean, this notarized copy is a very real form of identification. The irony is that the more practical legislation applicable to daily life, like parking or hiring maids, is often conveniently ignored or circumscribed.

— *Chapter Four* —

FAMILY COMES FIRST

If you arrive in Chile with any preconceived ideas about women's roles and machismo in Latin America, you may be pleasantly surprised, as we were, to find that women have a great deal of influence and are very active in almost all aspects of Chilean society. A much closer look, however, reveals that in spite of the significant advances women have made, many are content, or are required to continue to play traditional roles.

WOMEN IN THE WORKFORCE

Many women participate in the workforce, either for personal development, financial reasons or both. In 1996, over 36 percent of all women worked outside the home. This number was slightly higher in urban areas, but dropped to 20 percent in rural areas. What is more impressive, however, is that between 1990 and 1996 the number of women entering the workforce increased at a faster pace than the number of men. Yet, while over 50 percent of women in the highest income bracket were employed, only 19 percent of the women in the lowest income bracket were employed. Many of these women had jobs as workers, secretaries or domestic helpers.

POVERTY

As in most countries, women and children tend to suffer from poverty at a higher rate than men and Chile is no exception. In 1996, 23.5 percent of all Chilean women lived in poverty. While this is a significant number, it is down from 39.3 percent in 1990. Hit especially hard are the families headed by women. In 1996, 22 percent of all homes in the country were headed by a woman. The percentage of such families living in poverty was slightly less than the percentage of families with a male head of household. Among the indigent poor, however, the percentage was 5.5 for female heads of households versus 4.7 for male heads of households, down from 11.9 percent and 10.3 percent respectively, in 1990.

EDUCATION

Women in Chile, on the whole, do not lag far behind men in terms of education. On average, women over the age of 35 have spent under one full year less time in school than men. Women under 35 either have equal or more education than men. The average woman in the lowest income bracket completes 7.3 years of school, while women in the highest income bracket jump to 12.4 years.

MIDDLE AND UPPER-CLASS WOMEN

Well-educated women from higher income brackets are not only employed in the traditional fields of nursing, teaching and social services, but also as doctors, dentists, lawyers, engineers and economists. Women have also been integrated into the armed services, although they do not serve alongside men in combat. Yet, there are few industry leaders, and women are under-represented in politics. There are only a few female elected officials and one leader of a political party. In recent history there has never been more than two or three female cabinet ministers out of about 20 cabinet members. One area where women are gaining ground is in the running of government regulatory agencies.

While many Chilean women work, studies have found that they work in lower-paying jobs. This is even more apparent in the highest income bracket where women earn barely more than half what men earn. This situation improves slightly for the lowest income bracket where women bring in about 70 percent of men's incomes. This trend holds true when the level of education is constant. Chilean women have made great strides entering fields that were once dominated by men. However, even in these positions women do not receive equal pay for equal work and often reach a glass ceiling.

SOCIAL SERVICES

The government and the business community provide more social services for women, especially working mothers, than even some developed countries. The Chilean government established the Servicio Nacional de la Mujer or SERNAM (National Office for Women) in 1990. The director is a member of the Cabinet. Its goals are to promote women's involvement in society and to improve the lives of women in a wide range of areas. It addresses such issues as discrimination, job opportunities, education, family development, health, domestic violence, self-esteem building, housing and social and political participation. Currently, Chilean law states that a women is to receive three months paid maternity leave and cannot be fired from her job due to pregnancy. Mothers (and now fathers) are eligible for unpaid leave if a child becomes seriously ill. Depending upon the size of a company and the percentage of women employed, the company must provide nursery care. The company can either set up its own nursery or hire an independent firm to provide the service.

NANAS

Working mothers in Chile are not faced with the same problems that they are in some developed countries. Because labor is relatively cheap, many upper, middle and even some lower-class families hire *nanas* (nannies) or *empleadas* who not only look after the children but also clean, cook and do the laundry. The *nana* is a trusted partner in raising the children and her presence is a great source of relief. Many middle and upper-class families have live-in *nanas* who are available at almost any hour if need be. Most women from the lower income bracket turn to their extended family, friends, neighbors or even older children for help with young children. Day care centers are another option. Many low income neighborhoods have facilities available and offices usually have some sort of arrangement with a day care center.

TRADITIONAL VALUES

Although the statistics present a society where women have made great strides, a closer look reveals that many women continue to adhere to traditional values. We have met many young professional women who appeared to have very promising careers, yet gave it all up to get married and raise a family. There are many bright women who tell you outright that they are only studying at the university or working in order to find a good husband. Although women are gaining some level of independence, there is still a great deal of pressure for them to marry. Many cannot wait to be addressed as Señora (Mrs.) instead of Señorita (Miss) because of the respect it commands. How can these contradictions be explained?

Certainly these attitudes cannot be blamed on machismo. For, although Chilean society can be described as conservative and traditional, there is no blatant machismo. When machismo rears its ugly head in Chile it is very subtle. While there may be exceptions, Chilean men for the most part are not opposed to having their wives work. In fact, not only does the extra income help, but many men are proud of their wives and their abilities.

The best explanation is that for all the advancements in employment opportunities, Chilean women still regard family as the most important aspect of their lives. In the northern hemisphere, women once sacrificed their families to have careers, and the pendulum is now swinging back, placing more emphasis on home life. Chilean women, in general, never followed that route. Family always came first, and in that sense, women have managed to maintain a degree of control and power in society.

FAMILY LIFE

In spite of the forward-looking approach most Chileans have with respect to women in the workplace, family life continues to follow long-standing traditions that are only slowly being challenged. The family is the central and most important social unit in Chile and roles within it have not changed much over the last few years.

Raising Children

Young children are raised in a very relaxed manner. You'll notice that some parents beg their children to behave rather than demand it. There appears to be a general lack of discipline in public places. On numerous occasions we have wanted to sternly tell a child to sit down and be good because the parents' half-hearted attempts had been ineffectual. Yet once they reach adolescence they are, for the most part, very well behaved and respectful of their parents.

Ties That Bind

In the past, a woman who was single and lived on her own was assumed to be loose, bringing shame upon herself and her entire family. While this perception has changed and more and more women are moving out of their parents' home before marriage, the total number is still relatively small. Most single women in Santiago who live alone come from other cities and therefore have no family with which to live.

Family is still the number one priority in Chile.

Most children live at home until they get married because the concept of striking out on one's own is not as pervasive as it is in other cultures. If you are studying at any of the universities, you'll note that the majority of the students live at home. There is no dorm life. Thus, there is no defining moment for establishing one's independence before marriage. This is also due, in part, to the high level of support given by the family, both financial and otherwise. Most students or newly employed young adults cannot afford their own apartment, and there is no pressure from either family or friends to move out. In many cases, mom (or the nana) continues doing the laundry, cooking, cleaning, ironing, etc. Why would anyone want to leave?

The Regalón

The term *regalón/regalona* refers to someone who is spoiled by one or both parents. Each family has at least one. Don't get this confused, however, with a spoiled brat who acts snotty and is given whatever he or she wants. The term has a positive connotation and refers more to pampering. Even if the child doesn't ask to be catered to, the parents will do so out of love.

SOCIAL LIFE

As recently as a few years ago, women would not venture out to the bars or discos if not in the company of a man, whether as part of a couple or group. Women did not even go out on the town alone in large numbers because this was viewed as scandalous and inappropriate behavior. However, this is changing and you will now see groups of women out at the discos together. Along with this new sense of independence, there is a growing demand for respect and equality. In a recent well-publicized case five women successfully sued a restaurant for discrimination.

In spite of the social changes, chivalry is alive and well. When women and men go out for the evening, whether as friends or as a couple, the women are often escorted home. Santiago is no less safe than most large cities, so this is not done purely for safety reasons, it is just considered gentlemanly behavior.

When women and men go out together in groups as friends, the women may or may not be expected to pay for themselves. If a woman is invited out on a date with a man, she will not be expected to pay at all. Chilean women will not offer to pay, but if a foreign woman insists on paying, the man will politely but adamantly refuse her request.

POLOLOS

Dating in Chile is a very serious undertaking. Single Chileans either have a *pololo* (boyfriend) or *polola* (girlfriend) or are not seeing anyone. It is not common for Chileans to date casually or to date more than one person at a time. The word "pololo" comes from the name of a bug that buzzes around people incessantly.

The majority of couples meet through friends, at school or at work. By the time they finally go out in a romantic setting, it is fairly clear that a serious relationship is being formed. Once a couple is officially a couple the relationship becomes very intense and possessive. Couples will likely spend all their free time together. If they see their friends, they do so as a couple. It is rare that either would go out with just the girls or just the guys.

Coming from a different culture, this could be viewed as very suffocating and could be one explanation for the relatively high number of annulled marriages and adulterous affairs. The choice appears to be either to have no romantic life at all or to enter into a very serious relationship. There is no middle road.

Couples tend to be very affectionate in public. Young couples hold hands, embrace and kiss passionately whether at a restaurant, the movies, or just out walking around. If you come from a more reserved country you will have to get used to this practice. Some couples can be particularly hard to ignore, but giving them dirty looks will not cause them to change their behavior. Because most young couples live at home, they have no private areas where they can be intimate. As a result, parks, particularly Santa Lucia Hill or Parque Forestal in Santiago, have become a meeting place for countless amorous couples. In fact, in the small town of Pichidangui, there is a space among the rocks along the coastline commonly known as *la cuna* (the cradle). It is a comfortable space for two people to lie in without being seen. The name refers to the number of babies conceived here.

YOUNG BRIDES AND GROOMS

Chileans tend to marry within the same socio-economic class. They also marry young. Although a small number of liberal Chileans are beginning to live together before marriage, this is still relatively uncommon.

Most Chileans marry in their 20s. In the past, women were under a great deal of pressure to marry before their 30th birthday, when they would be labeled old maids. When Susan turned 30 in Chile, everyone's first question upon learning her age was "And you've never been married?" They found it easier to believe that she had married and divorced than to believe she had never married.

STARTING A FAMILY

Chileans tend to have children relatively soon after marriage. Since the family is the most important social unit, very few couples opt not to have children. It might seem surprising then that Chile has a very low birthrate compared to other developing countries. Most middle-class families have only two or three children. Wealthier and poorer families tend to be bigger.

Abortion is illegal in Chile due to the strong influence of the Roman Catholic Church. However, Chile has one of the highest abortion rates in Latin America. In spite of the availability of contraceptives, abortion is used as a form of birth control. The birth control pill is sold over the counter at pharmacies without a prescription.

While the pill is relatively inexpensive, the cost is still prohibitive for lower income sectors. Condoms are sold only in drug stores and the variety is very limited.

SINGLE MOTHERS AND ILLEGITIMACY

Many pregnant, unwed women decide to keep their babies. Most continue to live at home and work, relying a great deal upon the support (emotional, financial and physical) of their families. While the social stigma associated with illegitimacy is slowly disappearing, current laws still treat these children differently, especially in terms of inheritance rights. The issue is currently being debated in Congress. Supporters and opponents of legislation that would rescind the distinction have raised arguments based on economic, legal, social and moral grounds.

FAMILY GATHERINGS

Due to the high value placed on family ties, many Chilean families are tightly knit and spend a great deal of time together. Susan had a glimpse of family life in Chile with her host family. The family consisted of six adult children, three married and three single, who still lived at home. Everyday a crowd descended upon the house for lunch. At least three of the children – sometimes accompanied by spouses – would come home from school or work to eat lunch together. In the evenings, it was not uncommon for at least one of the married children to drop by to say hello on their way home from work. And, of course, weekends saw the family united for a delicious meal and amusing conversation. Unfortunately, due to the demands of a developing society, the majority of Chileans now cannot afford to spend as much time together as before, but the family remains the number one priority.

The family does not consist of only the immediate children and grandchildren, but embraces cousins, aunts and uncles. On special occasions, such as birthdays and holidays, the entire family comes together. More importantly, the extended family serves as a support network. Although Chile has a high percentage of poverty, there is little homelessness, the main reason being that family takes in members who have fallen on hard times. Many Chilean households, especially the poorest, take in *allegados* (from the word "allegar," which means to put in close proximity), giving those in dire need the opportunity to get back on their feet.

ANNULMENTS

Chile suffers from a relatively high number of annulments. Divorce remains illegal, due mainly to the strong opposition of the Catholic Church. When a marriage breaks down, a couple requests an annulment of the civil marriage. This is not to be confused with an annulment of the religious marriage granted by the Catholic Church, which is a completely separate act and not as common. Because divorce is not an option, couples can either separate legally (but be prohibited from remarrying in Chile) or have the marriage annulled. Civil marriage annulment is obtained with the aid of attorneys who argue that there has been a procedural error in the civil marriage ceremony. Generally, witnesses testify, either truthfully or falsely, to facts that nullify the original proceedings. The standard claim is that either the bride or groom did not reside where they stated they did. One very important aspect of annulments is that they require the agreement of both parties. In particularly bitter separations, one party may refuse an annulment, preventing the other from ever remarrying.

Because a lawyer must be hired to process the request for an annulment, the poor are unable to legally terminate a marriage. Thus, when a couple separates, neither party can remarry under Chilean law. As a result, there are a large number of new families with no legal status. The Family Law Bill, which would legalize divorce, is currently being discussed in Congress. While most Chileans believe that divorce will eventually be legalized, the change is not expected in the immediate future.

Chapter Five

A POWERFUL CHURCH

Latin America is perceived by the outside world as being one of the great strongholds of the Roman Catholic Church. This is valid to a certain extent throughout the region and especially in Chile due to the early introduction of Catholicism.

Of what consequence was the introduction of Catholicism in Chile? The Catholic Church had absolute power over education and civil and canonical law. Even after independence from Spain, the 1833 constitution declared the Roman Catholic Church the official church of Chile. Until the early 20th century, priests used their position to reinforce the existing economic and political order. In sermons, for example, they told farm laborers that obedience and submission to authority were virtues that should guide their lives. Eventually, the relationship between church and state became difficult. By the 1880s most of the privileges the church had enjoyed had been revoked by the state.

Church affiliation has been on the decrease since the 1970s. Approximately 15 percent of the population declared themselves Protestant in the 1992 census, about 90 percent of whom belong to Pentecostal (Evangelical) denominations.

NON-CHRISTIANS

In 1992, a significant minority of Chileans (about 7 percent) declared themselves to be indifferent to religion, more than double the number in 1970. Other religious groups, such as Jews, Muslims and Greek Orthodox accounted for 4.2 percent of the population. Protestant and other denominations have not had a very strong political identity or important leadership roles in political or social life until now.

The Jewish community is strong, powerful and tightly knit, but is practically invisible in Chile. Most Chileans do not know that Don Francisco, Chile's most famous television host, is Jewish and would be surprised to find out. Chileans tend to think of Jews in terms of the Holocaust or Orthodox Judaism, and not in terms of people on the street. There is a high concentration of Jews in academia, research, the judiciary and the arts in Chile.

The number of Muslims is very small and they come primarily from the Palestinian community.

PROTESTANT GROUPS

Chile has a greater number of Protestants than do many other predominantly Roman Catholic countries in Latin America. Some are Anglicans and Lutherans, the descendants of British and German immigrants who came to Chile in the 19th century. Most belong to "fundamentalist" churches, which emphasize a direct reading of the Bible. Often Protestants are more enthusiastic in the profession of their faith, perhaps as a result of their being mostly converts. While a quarter of adult Chileans attend church services at least once a week, 46 percent of Protestants versus 18 percent of Roman Catholics are regular churchgoers. Among practicing Protestants, more than half come from lower socio-economic groups. For decades surveys indicated that less than 10 percent of the working class could be considered practicing Catholics. It is among this previously unresponsive group that the Protestant movement has gained the most ground.

Pentecostals

In Chile the Pentecostal movements are generally called *evangélicos*, as a broad category. The name Canutos has also stuck, after the name of one of their early leaders. On Sunday you may see groups in the streets carrying large Bibles with guitars and accordions. Along the way they sing and recite Bible verses in unison and a leader or perhaps a recent convert may speak using a portable loudspeaker.

Pentecostals and other Protestant groups are becoming very involved with the media to spread their message. They have been buying radio and television air time to promote their views, gain members and raise money. This follows the American televangelist model, as many of the groups in Chile are based in the US.

Mormons

The Church of Jesus Christ Latter Day Saints, also known as the Mormon Church, is another of the fastest growing Protestant sects in Chile. There is now a Mormon temple in practically every town throughout Chile. The church supports an aggressive outreach program, carried out by missionaries canvassing door-to-door. The church also provides full scholarships for university study in the US.

CHILEAN CATHOLICISM

The Virgin Mary

A very important religious figure in Latin America is the Virgin Mary. She is believed to intervene in desperate cases and plead for mercy before God. Her popularity is very strong as a result and there are numerous shrines to the Virgin Mother. There is a huge statue of Mary atop the San Cristóbal Hill which overlooks Santiago. It is especially beautiful at night when it is bathed in light. The Virgin Mary, widely worshiped as the Virgen del Carmen, is also the patron of the Chilean armed forces. Mary is also worshiped as the Virgen de Andacollo, Virgen de la Tirana, and the Virgen de lo Vasquez, among others.

Practicing the Faith

There are several yearly pilgrimages and processions to Catholic churches in Chile that include special images of the Virgin or saints. On the Feast of Saint Peter, statues are taken out of local churches, placed in fishing boats and floated around the fishing grounds to ensure a good catch.

In the Chilean countryside and alongside most roads and highways it is common to see shrines called *animitas* marking the place of death of a loved one. Candles are lit in remembrance and flowers may be laid at the site. Deceased family members may also be called upon in prayers to intercede on a relative's behalf.

Suffering in exchange for forgiveness is a common concept in Chilean Catholicism. Worshipers can often be seen "walking" down the aisle of the church on their knees, begging for mercy. On the Feast of the Immaculate Conception, Santiaguinos walk to the Santuario de lo Vasquez, a church 86 kilometers (53 miles) away, seeking absolution for their sins or fulfilling a promise for a favor granted.

Chinos are brotherhoods that call themselves guardians of the Virgin Mary. These groups are common in northern and central Chile

77

Animitas, *shrines dedicated to deceased loved ones, are a common sight along the highways of Chile.*

and in Bolivia and Peru. In spite of their name, which means "the Chinese," their practices have nothing to do with Chinese culture. In fact these societies wear special uniforms that resemble those of conquistadors, Indians or ancient Romans. They are known for dancing and chants of the divinity that resemble prayers sung in Spain during religious festivals.

The Pope

Pope John Paul II visited Chile in 1987, during the military regime. Some felt that he should not have gone because it would validate the dictatorship. Others argued that religion has nothing to do with politics. He traveled quite extensively throughout the country and inspired many with his presence. In Puerto Montt, he crossed the bay in a fishing boat. He visited low income areas, where he stressed the teachings of Christ, the virtues of charity and the power of love. The saying "Love is stronger" ("el amor es mas fuerte") often heard in Chile was originally part of his sermon.

It may come as a surprise that despite being a Catholic country the Catholic Church in Chile suffers from a shortage of priests. Around half of the 2,500 priests in Chile are foreign born.

Santa Teresa de los Andes

Born in 1900 in Santiago to parents of great wealth, Juanita Fernández Solar, or Santa Teresa, entered the Carmelite convent in the city of Los Andes at the age of 18. She took the name Teresa in honor of the Spanish Saint Teresa of Jesus whom she admired. A weak girl, she became very ill and died one year later. A number of posthumous miracles have been accredited to Teresa and she was beatified in 1987 and finally canonized in 1993. Her canonization represents the power of prayers and faith.

Padre Hurtado

Chileans are proudly looking forward to having a second saint sometime in the near future. Alberto Hurtado (1902–1952), known in Chile as Padre Hurtado, was an energetic Jesuit priest who placed great importance upon helping those in need. He had an old pick-up truck and was known for driving throughout Santiago, rescuing homeless children. He took them to the home he had founded, Hogar de Cristo (the House of Christ). He died of cancer at a young age, but remains a very powerful figure in Chile especially among the young. His life's main work, Hogar de Cristo, is the most successful charitable organization in Chile. Many consider him to have been a living saint.

POLITICS AND THE CATHOLIC CHURCH

The Roman Catholic Church played a key role in the defense of human rights in the wake of the 1973 military coup. The church was a supporter of the restoration of democracy and church lawyers provided legal defense for prisoners. Before the coup, the church feared Allende might use schools to indoctrinate the students with Marxist philosophy. The coup was therefore initially welcomed, and church leaders gave validity to the military *junta* by officiating at ceremonies.

Under Pinochet, the church created a degree of opposition and provided protection for a number of non-governmental organizations, winning it credibility as a modern social force. After the restoration of democracy, under orders from Rome, the church became more apolitical. But in reward for the support of democracy, church leaders made it clear that they counted upon the new government for support of their conservative agenda, the basic tenets of which are opposition to divorce and abortion.

One example of the church's strong influence on government was the banning of the movie "The Last Temptation of Christ." This decision was challenged, and, in a divided but final decision, the courts upheld the ban, arguing that the movie offends the Catholic Church.

RITUALS

Many of the rituals that Chileans observe are religious in nature and are based on long-standing traditions. Due to the fact that a majority of Chileans are Catholic, most rituals stem from the Holy Sacraments. Even Chileans who do not attend church services on a regular basis celebrate major events in the church, such as baptisms, weddings and funerals.

Baptism

When a child is approximately six months old it will be baptized. In the cities, this is a relatively quiet affair. The child is baptized by a priest in the parent's parish church and two very close family members or friends serve as the *padrinos de bautismo* (godparents). Following the church service, all guests proceed to the family's home for a long lunch or tea.

In rural areas, however, the baptism of a newborn can be a much more elaborate affair. The event can last the entire day, beginning with an *asado* (a Chilean style barbeque). The food and drinks are abundant and the atmosphere is festive.

Gifts are given when a child is baptized. They may be religious in nature or not. In Chile, baby showers are generally not given for expectant mothers. It is customary to just give a gift when the child is born.

First Communion

A child receives his or her First Communion around the age of eight. The child is guided by *padrinos de comunión*, close friends or family members chosen by the parents. Boys dress up in suits and girls wear white dresses with veils. Following the church service lunch or tea is served at the family's home and gifts are given. Once again they may be religious in nature or not.

Birthdays

Chileans celebrate birthdays with parties or small family gatherings. Young children normally will be given parties at home with cousins and/or friends. However, with the growing number of fast food outlets, children's parties are increasingly held at McDonald's or Chuck E. Cheese (a pizza parlor with games and shows for children). Adults usually celebrate at someone's home. Gifts are opened during the party after the cake is cut. If attending a birthday party, always bring a gift, even if it is just a small token. When the host dims the lights you know it's time for the cake to be brought out. Everyone sings the Chilean version of "Happy Birthday to You." So that you can sing along, the words are as follows: "Cumpleaños Feliz; Te deseamos a ti; Feliz Cumpleaños (name); Que los cumplas feliz."

Saints' Days

In addition to birthdays, Chileans celebrate their Saint's Day. Each saint is honored on a certain day of the year according to the Catholic calendar and Chileans celebrate the day of the Saint for whom they are named. This practice is kept mainly by older Chileans. However,

Chileans named after very popular saints, such as Pedro (Peter) and Pablo (Paul) celebrate their Saint's Day regardless of their age. Those who observe their Saint's Day do so in a manner similar to that of celebrating a birthday. There are cakes and presents at a small party or family gathering.

WEDDINGS

In Chile, the civil marriage, or legal aspect of the union, is completely separate from the religious ceremony. Everyone must be married in a civil ceremony and only those who wish to have the marriage consecrated by the church participate in a religious ceremony. Couples who have two ceremonies celebrate the date of the religious ceremony as their wedding anniversary.

Civil Ceremony

Everyone wishing to be married under Chilean law must be married by an official from the Civil Registry. This is a short ceremony, approximately 15 minutes long, in the Civil Registry offices during the week. After scheduling an appointment, the couple arrives at the office with two witnesses, usually family members or close friends. The official performs the ceremony, verifying the identity of the bride and groom and providing a legal explanation of what marriage entails.

At this time, the official asks how the couple wishes to be married. In Chile, there are three different legal forms of marriage: 1) Comunidad de Bienes (Community Property) – According to this type of marriage all property is considered jointly owned; 2) Separación de Bienes (Divided Property) – Under this type of marriage what each person owns and earns remains separate property. This is the form most often chosen; 3) Assets acquired prior to marriage remain separate, while those acquired during the marriage become common property. Because this last form of marriage is fairly new, the ramifications remain somewhat unclear.

Although the law in Chile requires just a civil ceremony, many couples only consider themselves truly married after the religious ceremony.

After the couple gives their consent to be married, they sign the civil registry records and are given a Libreta de Familia (Family Book). The marriage of the couple is recorded legally in this book which also has pages to record the birth and death of any children and the deaths of the husband and wife. This *libreta* is independent of any certificate, but summarizes the history of the family. In addition to being a useful tool in completing transactions, such as school registration, it is an important symbol, because it is proof of a formal, legal relationship.

In most families, it is the woman who guards the *libreta* because it is a source of pride and gives legal status to her family. A common joke says that women will only sleep with a man "con libreta" (with the book).

The civil ceremony is very simple, the men wear suits and the women wear dresses, not bridal gowns. The offices are small, so only the couple, the witnesses and maybe the parents are present. Following the ceremony, the couple, accompanied by family and intimate friends enjoy a celebratory lunch.

Religious Ceremony

As little as a few days to as many as a few months following the civil ceremony, the couple may be married in a religious service. Most weddings are held in the evening, around 8:00 p.m., on a Saturday. In the Catholic Church a full mass is not celebrated, just a short 20 minute wedding ceremony with Communion. In Chile, there are no "wedding parties," i.e. bridesmaids or groomsmen. Instead, the bride and groom are each accompanied by *padrinos de matrimonio* – a *madrina* (a woman) and a *padrino* (a man) who stand beside them and pledge to support them in their future life together. Most often the parents are asked to be the *padrinos de matrimonio*. However, if a parent is absent, another close relative or close friend may be asked.

Chileans never give money as a wedding gift. This would imply that no thought was given to selecting a present for the newlyweds. Even gift certificates are considered inappropriate. Most couples receive traditional wedding gifts, mainly household items. Increasingly couples are registering at major department stores for specific gifts to make it easier for their guests. These stores publish Listas de Novios (engaged couples lists) in the paper on a regular basis.

FUNERALS

Following a death, a wake and funeral will be held at the church on the same day. Because the body is not normally embalmed, the funeral is held shortly after the death. Very close friends and extended family often arrive at the church a few hours prior to the service to provide support. The immediate family will observe a certain period of external mourning, but this practice is more obvious in the country-side and among very traditional families. Today, it is a matter of personal choice to dress in black for an extended period.

One month following the death of a loved one and then every year on the anniversary of the death, a full Catholic mass may be offered in the deceased's memory. Other families may opt to offer their prayers in silence. On November 1, All Saints' Day, family members go to the cemetery to visit the grave of a loved one.

In the past, the remains were interred in mausoleum type concrete blocks. Only the wealthy could afford graves in the ground. A common practice was to remove the remains of a spouse from the mausoleum after a period of time, place them in an urn and return them to the mausoleum. This allowed both spouses to be buried together. Newer cemeteries mostly offer graves in the ground.

Many people send flowers when a person has died to offer their condolences. A growing number of people now prefer to make a donation to charity in memory of the deceased. The charity then sends a sympathy card with the name of the donor to the family. An obituary is placed in the paper to announce a person's death. Friends may take out their own notices in the paper to remember the deceased.

In rural areas funerals can be a much more involved affair. The wake itself can last for a few days, either at the deceased's home or the local church. Many mourners bring food and the eating continues until the funeral takes place. In the event that a baby has died, the mourners sometimes hold a Velorio del Angelito (Little Angel's Wake). It is widely believed that the baby will go straight to heaven, so it cannot be a mournful event.

Chapter Six

FIESTAS AND FOLKLORE

TRIGG

FIESTAS

Chileans are a religious and patriotic people. Of the 14 official holidays celebrated each year in Chile, half are religious. Religious holidays are observed privately and quietly while secular holidays are celebrated with much fanfare.

New Year

New Year's Eve is a very festive occasion. It takes place in the middle of the summer and is celebrated with *asados* (barbeques) and family gatherings. Many Santiaguinos spend this holiday at the beach. At midnight fireworks light up the skies throughout the country, with several displays in Santiago alone. The most spectacular fireworks display explodes over the Pacific Ocean in Valparaíso. The show

Many Chileans celebrate fiestas such as New Year's with a family barbeque.

attracts immense crowds and many people arrive early in the afternoon to secure a prime viewing spot. At the stroke of midnight people embrace to wish each other a Happy New Year. Many Chileans eat a spoonful of lentils for good luck. Others put money and bus or plane tickets in their pockets to ensure wealth and travel in the coming year. After celebrating the stroke of midnight at home with the family, many people visit friends until the wee hours of the morning.

Carnival
Carnival is a celebration of excess prior to the abstinence of Lent. The current festival is a blend of Aymara Indian and Catholic traditions now observed by Indians and non-Indians alike. Carnival is celebrated in the Chilean Altiplano and is heavily influenced by carnivals in Bolivia and Peru. It is not practiced in central or southern Chile.

Semana Santa
Many Chileans attend church during Holy Week, which culminates with Easter Sunday. Good Friday is an official holiday and offices are

closed. During Holy Week children pull dolls representing Judas around the neighborhood in little carts. They visit houses asking for coins to symbolize the money Judas received for betraying Jesus. At the end of the day, the doll is burned.

Easter Sunday is the holiest day for Catholics and many Chileans spend the day in their homes with their families. Chileans of German descent traditionally celebrate the day with Easter egg hunts. Recently this custom has spread to the rest of society.

Cuasimodo

Cuasimodo is observed on the Sunday following Easter Sunday. It is a very important festival celebrated throughout the entire central region of Chile. The local priest, riding in a carriage, leads a procession through the community, administering Communion to the homebound. The priest is accompanied by hundreds of *huasos* (Chilean cowboys) riding horses and carrying religious images. The *huasos* wear traditional dress but remove their hats and tie kerchiefs around their heads as a sign of respect. The festival originated in the 1800s when *huasos* accompanied priests traveling through sparsely populated areas to protect them from thieves. Today, however, many participants ride bicycles decorated with brightly colored paper and streamers instead of horses.

Navy Day

May 21 is Navy Day, the second most important patriotic holiday in Chile. This day honors the heroism and courage of Arturo Prat, the Chilean Navy's main hero. May 21 is the anniversary of the Battle of Iquique, which took place in 1879 during the War of the Pacific. Captain Prat, outnumbered and certain to be defeated by Peruvian ships, refused to surrender. He and his crew members died fighting after boarding the enemy vessel. News of this act of bravery served as a catalyst for the Chilean people and was a turning point in the war, which Chile eventually won.

Arturo Prat, Chile's foremost naval hero, is honored each year on May 21.

The president makes an annual "State of the Nation" address on this day as Congress opens for a new session. The Mensaje Presidencial recounts the achievements of the past year and lays out the administration's future plans for the country. The speech is aired live on television and radio.

Festival de San Pedro

On June 29, or the first Sunday following, the tiny fishing village of Horcón, about 150 kilometers (93 miles) north of Santiago, celebrates the festival of San Pedro (Saint Peter). All the fishing boats, as well as the village, are gaily decorated. Musical groups called *chinos* from Horcón and other nearby villages dance in devotion to the patron saint of fishermen, while an image of Saint Peter is carried around the bay. It is believed that Saint Peter will bless them with bountiful fish harvests. Similar festivities are held in many other coves along the Chilean coast.

La Tirana

The festival of La Tirana is celebrated for three days each July in La Tirana, a village 70 kilometers (43 miles) from the city of Iquique. During the festival the population swells from 5,000 to over 70,000. La Tirana has been strongly influenced by the Bolivian Carnival celebrations, particularly the one in Oruro.

The village is named after an Incan princess who was converted to Catholicism by her Spanish lover. She was the daughter of the high priest of the Sun Temple in Cuzco, although she lived in what is now Chile. After watching her father murdered by conquistadors, she killed any Spaniard who came near her or her people and gained the nickname of La Tirana de Tamarugal (the Tyrant of Tamarugal).

One night a silver miner named Vasco de Almeida was captured. It had been the rule to kill all Spaniards, but the princess fell in love with him, and through him learned the Christian concept of eternal life after death. She converted to Christianity in order to be united forever with de Almeida in the next life.

The princess was baptized with the name María. Soon after, she imposed Catholicism on her people by force. María and her husband were eventually killed by angry mobs. As she lay dying, she begged to be buried with her husband at the place where she had been baptized. The grave was marked with a cross.

Years later a priest found the cross, and upon hearing the legend built a temple in honor of the Virgen del Carmen of La Tirana. This sanctuary is the end point of the festival procession.

11 de Septiembre

September 11 was declared a holiday by the military regime to commemorate the day Allende was removed from power in a military coup. With the restoration of democracy, it became a flashpoint marked by protests. In 1998, Congress agreed to abolish the holiday and replace it with a National Day of Unity celebrated on the first Monday of September.

Fiestas Patrias

Fiestas Patrias is a two-day holiday: September 18 is National Day and September 19 is Army Day. Many Chileans prepare *asados* at home during the day and visit the *fondas* at night. *Fondas* are fairs set up all over the country with tents serving food such as *empanadas* (meat or cheese filled turnovers), *anticuchos* (shish kebabs), *carne asada* (grilled beef and pork) and drinks, such as *chicha* (fermented grape punch) and *pisco* (grape brandy). Many of the larger tents feature live music and dancing. The national dance of Chile is the *cueca*, danced continuously during National Day. If you go to a *fonda*, no doubt you will be invited to dance the *cueca*. Don't be shy, it's a fun and easy way of showing Chileans how much you enjoy their country. Also popular during this time of year are the Chilean-style rodeos.

Army Day is celebrated with a large military parade at Parque O'Higgins. The parade is televised live on all channels and lasts about four hours. Every division of the Armed Forces is represented. There is an unofficial competition among the baton leaders of each of the four military academies to see who can goose-step the highest. Other highlights include the army mountain troops, dressed in white uniforms complete with skis strapped across their back and commandos brandishing their *corvos*, knives especially designed to disembowel an adversary. These troops invaded southern Peru during the War of the Pacific and became notorious for the use of these knives. Even today mothers in southern Peru warn their children not of the boogie man, but of the terrible Chilean.

September is a festive month owing to these two very important holidays. Chileans are bursting with national pride and the flag is flown throughout the country (the only month when this is allowed). Kites suddenly appear and are sold on every street corner. Kite-flying competitions are held and some of the *comisiones* or battles can be fierce. The strings are coated with pulverized glass and the objective is to cut loose your opponent's kite.

Chilean children take advantage of September's spring breezes and the festive atmosphere with kites and pinwheels.

All Saints' Day

On November 1, many Chileans visit the cemetery to pay their respects to the dead. When this holiday falls near the weekend, it also signals the unofficial beginning of summer. Santiaguinos flock to the beach for the first time following a cold damp winter.

Immaculate Conception

Catholics celebrate the Immaculate Conception on December 8. A number of Chileans make pilgrimages on this day. One of the biggest pilgrimages entails walking from Santiago to the Santuario de la Virgen de lo Vasquez 86 kilometers (53 miles) away. The Santuario de lo Vasquez is a shrine to the Blessed Virgin on the main highway between Santiago and the twin cities of Viña del Mar and Valparaíso. Many people stop to visit the shrine throughout the year because it is believed that all prayers to the Virgen de lo Vasquez will be answered. There is a wall in the courtyard covered with plaques thanking and praising the Virgin Mary for answering their petitions. Most children receive their First Communion on this day.

Christmas

In Chile, Christmas is a much more relaxed holiday than in other parts of the world. There is a Christmas spirit, but one is not overwhelmed with Christmas decorations, except in the shopping malls. Santa Claus makes his appearance, dying in the summer Santiago heat in his heavy, red suit. Chileans adorn their homes with nativity scenes and Christmas trees, both real and artificial, a tradition brought to Chile by Germans. Christmas, like most holidays, is family oriented with an emphasis on children. Families attend midnight mass, and open presents on Christmas Eve. On Christmas Day families gather for an *asado* or spend the day at the beach. It is traditional to serve *pan de pascua* (Christmas Bread), which, unlike fruit cake in the US, is devoured immediately, and *cola de mono*, a Christmas liqueur.

FOLKLORE

Mapuche

Today the term "Mapuche" (people of the land) encompasses most of the peoples native to central Chile. The Mapuche originally lived on Chiloé Island and the surrounding mainland territories to the north and south in both Chile and Argentina. There were around 14 different tribal groups in Chile when the Spanish arrived. Some survive in small numbers, others have been eliminated entirely, the result of conquistadors, disease, and famine.

The majority of the native peoples in Chile are Mapuche, although Aymara live in the north. Census figures indicate that there are around 300,000 Mapuche living on reservations in southern Chile. An additional 1.3 million Chileans identify themselves as at least part Mapuche, many of whom have migrated to the cities looking for work.

Ethnically and linguistically the Mapuche were one people, but the vast length of their territory gave rise to differences in dialect and customs. Those on Chiloé were sedentary and monogamous fishermen and farmers, while those on the mainland were polygamous nomadic fishermen, farmers and herdsmen. The Mapuche believed that while they could own personal property, the land and the animals were for the common benefit of the clan.

Southern Chile was fairly densely populated by the Mapuche before the Spanish conquest. Early chronicles describe open lands with rolling hills. The forests were kept in check by the grazing livestock. However, after smallpox and war decimated the Mapuche, forests reclaimed the land.

The family head was called Cacique or Lonko, and could have as many as 10 wives as a sign of his power. The Mapuche lived in family groups of up to 500 members. The Caciques formed alliances with other family groups for trade, but there was no central government.

This, and the fact that they did not have permanent villages, saved the Mapuche from early subordination by the Spanish. While the society was ultimately led by men, medicine women, called Machi, were very powerful and as important to society as the Mapuche chiefs. Until today, women in general are held in high esteem and play a major role in their religion. According to Mapuche tradition, only women can communicate directly with the gods.

The spirituality of native Amerindians in general is profound, and the Mapuches are no exception. Although they have no temples, Mapuches believe that there are positive and negative forces present in every act. They look for divine intervention in all aspects of their lives. The significant forces of life, love and creation are represented by Ngenechen, while death and destruction are embodied in Wekufu. While the Mapuche accept that divine spirits are everywhere, they nevertheless believe in the existence of a supreme being called Guinechen (master of the land). The east represents the positive forces and therefore plays an important role in the lives of the Mapuche. In fact, Mapuche dwellings, called *rukas*, always face east.

One of the most well-known Mapuche festivals is Ngillatun. It is a prayer ceremony to invoke the spirit Pillan to ensure a good harvest. The Machi leads the ceremony and uses a *rewe* (ladder to heaven) that also faces east. The whole town participates with singing and dancing and in the past an animal was sacrificed. Participants paint their faces blue and white, sacred colors which hold positive meanings. Afterwards there is a big party and the Mapuches celebrate by eating and drinking lots of *chicha*.

Several unique instruments can be found in Mapuche culture. The *trutruka* is a very long (the end rests on the ground) sort of trumpet that makes a loud monotone noise. The Machi play the *cultrún*, a type of drum, during rituals. For sport the Mapuche play a game called *chueca*, which is similar to field hockey, using a wooden ball.

Every culture has its own explanation for the creation of the world. According to Mapuche legend, their land was formed when two snakes met while crawling across a flat land. Kai Kai was a terrific snake that scared other animals. Trey Trey had the respect of the animals, but they were not afraid of him. Eventually they met in battle. Kai Kai won, but his hissing created an ocean that threatened all life. To save himself and the other animals, Trey Trey piled mounds of earth into mountains. The animals that were not strong enough to climb up fell into the sea to become fish. The animals that climbed the highest and the fastest became humans. After the flood, the humans settled in the fertile valley between Trey Trey's mountains and Kai Kai's ocean, and they called themselves Mapuche. They believe that the frequent tremors in Chile are due to the thrashing snakes.

Of course, the Mapuches of modern Chile have evolved into a culture somewhat distinct from that of centuries ago. Even on the reservations the Chilean national culture has a firm foothold, mostly brought in by the extension of primary education. A survey of Mapuche on four southern reservations found that less than 10 percent were monolingual Mapuche, around 50 percent spoke both Spanish and Mapuche in their homes, and 40 percent spoke only Spanish. Almost all Mapuche under 30 are literate in Spanish.

Mapuche traditionally wear brightly colored handwoven clothes, which the women accessorize with the fine jewelry for which the Mapuche are known. However, today they generally wear western clothes when not on the reservations.

Mapuche are well known for their silver work and you can buy such items in Santiago and Temuco. They started using silver after the arrival of the Spanish, from whom they got the precious metal. The intricate pieces are related to their religious beliefs and are generally worn during rituals. Certain pieces are used as a safeguard against evil and/or as a symbol of fertility. Mapuche silversmiths make earrings, necklaces, pendants, *ponchon* (similar to a stick pin) and items to decorate the hair. The distinctive pieces are large and flat with tubes, chains and links.

Chiloé

The island of Chiloé is the richest part of Chile in terms of mythology and legends. Many are derived from Indian beliefs mixed with the Spanish-Christian tradition. Christian beliefs come into play with good fighting evil. The isolation and inclement weather of the island work to create this mysticism.

Ask a Chilean about Chiloé and they will tell you about *brujos* (wizards), who form a secret society. To be accepted as a member of a society, a candidate must kill a close relative and perform other evil acts, from which they acquire immense magical powers. *Brujos* can fly, but only when wearing a vest made out of the skin of a virgin turned inside out. If you are in Chiloé and accidentally put on your sweater inside out, Chileans will ask you if you are planning to fly.

Most mythological beings are associated with *brujos*: Invunche, the guardian of the *brujos'* lair, is a baby whose limbs have all been broken and whose orifices have been sealed. Caleuche, a mythological ship, is the vessel of the *brujos* that appears at night and aboard which they enjoy a never-ending party. Pincoya and Pincoy, Chiloé's sirens, are half fish, half human. Trauco, a gnome with no feet, is blamed for impregnating young, unwed women. A friend was staying with a family in Chiloé and the parent seriously spoke of the *trauco* which had gotten their young daughter pregnant. There are dozens of other legends and creatures and several books written on the subject.

A popular event in Chiloé is a *minga*, which brings the entire community together. In Chiloé, one of the most common *minga* is to move an entire house. The house is mounted on tree trunks and pulled by oxen to the new site. The house can even be moved across the sea! When the house has arrived at its new location, the owner treats everyone to lots of food and drink in appreciation. In other parts of Chile – as in many other parts of the world – harvest time calls for a "minga-like" event where the whole community helps each individual gather his or her crops.

Huasos

Huasos are Chilean cowboys. These cowboys are not limited to an existence in old western movies, their culture is alive and flourishing. The term *"huaso"* is believed to come from an Indian word for shoulders or haunches. As the Mapuche had never seen horses before the Spanish conquest, they originally assumed that the rider was attached to the horse between the shoulder and the haunch. Of course the Mapuche soon discovered the truth, and went on to become formidable horsemen themselves. *Huasos* live in the Central Valley where cattle are raised. This Huaso Zone begins in Santiago and extends southward.

Huasos usually work alone or with a few others tending the cattle. Their solitude is broken up by rodeo competitions (there are over 200 rodeo clubs in Chile). At first, these rodeos were an annual event when workers rounded up the cattle to count and brand the animals for sale. Eventually they evolved into a festival where animals were brought to the village main square and riders showed off their skills. Today they are a contest of skill in cattle herding. For the last 150 years or so rodeo has been a sport with definite rules. Unlike rodeos in other countries, there is no roping or riding of untamed bulls and calves.

The elegant *huaso* outfit seen at the rodeos is a Chilean version of the Andalusian traditional dress for men. On his head he wears a broad and flat rimmed hat made of straw in the summer, and felt in the winter. A basic white shirt and black or brown pin-striped trousers are the foundation for his outfit. Over the shirt a short brown or black jacket is worn. The rider's calves are sheathed in black leather leggings decorated with long leather tassels. These chaps are called *pierneras* (derived from the Spanish word for leg, *pierna*) and fit over the riding boots and pants. *Pierneras* are used to protect the *huaso*'s legs when riding through the thick brush of the Huaso Zone. The spurs on the boots have rowels or spiked discs used to prod the flanks of the horse to make it go faster. Traditionally, *huasos* wear a *poncho*, a colorful shoulder cape also called a *manta*, on top of all their clothing.

The *huaso* is part of a team, including a horse and a partner. The horses were brought by the Spanish and are unique to Chile – not too tall, yet strong and intelligent.

Before the actual rodeo begins the riders perform individual tests of agility. These tests are judged and scored. There is a series of exercises; first the *huaso* walks his mount on a loose rein to prove the gait of the horse, which should be constant, firm and rapid. Then the horse and rider gallop back and forth in a straight line making dramatic about-faces, which the horse should make by turning its body while on its hind legs. Figure eights and circles test the speed and handling of the horses. Just when the mount has become excited, it must calm down as the rider dismounts and walks several paces away. The horse must remain perfectly motionless or it loses points.

The *huaso* rodeo consists of only one event – calf-pinning. *Huasos* have elevated this competition to a complex art form. The *huaso* rodeo takes place in a 40-meter arena. This ring is divided into two parts, each called a *medialuna* or half-moon. The pair of *huasos* enter the *medialuna* and wait for the young bull. This calf, like the bulls at the *corridas* in Spain, is supposed to have never entered a *medialuna* before to safeguard the purity of its reactions.

Although the *huaso* team works together, they do not have equal responsibilities while attempting to pin the calf. One horseman must guide the calf around the *medialuna* while the other follows behind the calf pushing. The pair must herd the calf around the ring twice before pinning it against a specially marked area of the railing. Each rider has three turns to pin the calf against the timber fence. Then the riders change places and run in the opposite direction, repeating the performance in reverse.

A *huaso* rodeo makes for an excellent weekend outing. The day includes music and food, such as *empanadas*, along with much local color. Most Chilean rodeos are held between September and May.

Cueca

Cueca is the national dance of Chile. While Chileans may not like to admit to the fact, *cueca* is also danced in neighboring countries. There has been plenty of discussion on the origin of the *cueca*; Spain, Africa and Peru have been mentioned as possibilities. According to some, it came about in rebellion against the Spanish and was a symbol of republican life.

Most Chileans will tell you that *cueca* evokes the mating ritual of hens and roosters and there is a good basis for this observation. The *cueca* is a courtship dance, but for all the sensual interpretation, it does not seem to be a very sexy dance. *Cueca* is no *lambada* with erotic pelvic thrusts! The couple do not touch while dancing *cueca*.

You can recognize a *cueca* by the handkerchiefs that are elaborately waved above the couple's heads. The characteristics of the dance depend on the region, but generally the couple face each other and dance back and forth and around each other while waving the handkerchief. *Cueca* is usually accompanied by a guitar, and sometimes a harp, accordion, piano and tambourine. In the north, a brass or reed band is sometimes the accompaniment. The spectators keep time by clapping. It is typically danced on National Day or at folklore shows.

Tijerales

The *tijerales* custom is widespread throughout Chile. *Tijerales* is the Spanish word for the roof support structure of a building. On all construction sites, regardless of whether it is a small house in a rural area or a major skyscraper, when the *tijerales* has been completed a flag is placed on the roof. There is a pause in construction and a barbeque is held for all those involved. Completing the *tijerales* symbolizes that the final stage of construction has finally been reached.

Easter Island

Easter Island or Isla de Pascua is shrouded in mystery. A group of Polynesians first settled the island around AD 400, led there in bark canoes by Hotu Matua, the king. As the population grew, a clan society developed based upon the extended family. The family unit jointly owned and cultivated the land and each clan was led by a chief (*ariki*). Crop production required relatively little time and labor, which allowed the islanders to devote much time and energy to ceremonial activities. Priests, scribes and artists were important to cultural development.

Easter Island is most famous for its Moais, large stones carved in the shape of predominantly male heads and torsos. The Moais are thought to represent dead chiefs or gods. There are also over 300 large stone platforms thought to be altars, called *ahu*. They were used for burials, ancestor worship and to commemorate past chiefs. Some are astronomically aligned, indicating an advanced degree of knowledge.

Rongorongo is a hieroglyphic script that was found inscribed on many wooden tablets and staffs in 1864. It is the only indigenous Oceania script found to have existed before the 20th century. The glyphs themselves are very small, about 1 centimeter tall, and many represent humans, birds, fish and plants. Every other line is written upside down so that the tablet must be inverted to continue reading. By 1866, only two years later, most of the tablets had been burnt, hidden or used for boat planks or fishing lines. Today, only about 20 tablets remain and no one has been able to successfully decipher them.

The island was also home to thousands of petroglyphs. Most of these rock carvings depict birds, animals and birdmen. The birdman (Tangata Manu) figures prominently in Easter Island folklore. This creature has a bird's head and a man's body and holds an egg in one hand. The cult of the birdman originated near Orongo. He was said to be an earthly representative of the creator god called Makemake. Each spring, a contest was held between the clans. A representative swam from Orongo to Motu Nui, a small islet nearby. The goal was to find the first egg laid by the Namu Tara, a sacred bird. During the search, other members of the tribe made offerings and prayed to Makemake. The winner was the first person to swim back to Orongo and present his chief with the egg. This chief was then named "birdman" for the year and led a procession to Rano Raraku where he lived in seclusion and enjoyed the favor of Makemake.

The Pascuenses (the Spanish term for the islanders) are also known for their wood carvings, the most famous being the Moai Kavakava (image of ribs). The small statue depicts a bearded man with his ribs sticking out. It is believed to represent the spirits of dead ancestors, called Aku Aku. According to legend, Chief Tuu-ko-ihu saw two of these spirits one night and they later appeared to him in a dream.

The people of Easter Island tattooed almost any part of their bodies. Faces, necks, chests, abdomens, backs, and legs were adorned with geometrical designs, and human or bird forms.

The Rapa Nui relate the story of their arrival on the island through the use of a game using string figures. These are called *kai kai*. The player forms a figure using a piece of string and through different finger movements is able to alter the figure. Meanwhile, the player sings a song describing how the original settlers built boats, sailed across the ocean to Rapa Nui and then dismantled the boats to build their first homes.

When the first Europeans arrived they did not find a flourishing civilization. Instead, they found a culture in decline. It is believed that as the society grew and developed, the island's population reached 7,000. However, this growth placed a heavy burden on the island's ecosystem. The island had been almost completely forested when the first settlers arrived. Land was continuously cleared for agricultural purposes, for fuel and to build houses and canoes. Most importantly, however, large tree trunks had been used to move the giant Moais across the island after they had been carved. Deforestation caused soil erosion and crops were insufficient to feed the large population.

The islanders were forced to live in caves and the lack of wood meant that no canoes could be built. They were trapped on an island which could no longer provide for them. The clans turned upon each other and were forced into cannibalism. It is believed that the Moais were knocked down during these wars.

When the Europeans arrived, the island was treeless. The population had already dwindled but the Peruvian slave raids in the 1860s and diseases introduced by the Europeans such as smallpox reduced the number of people by 90 percent. By 1877 only 111 people remained. The king, his son and the priests had all been captured as slaves. Without them, the Europeans were unable to learn about the island's culture and history. This led to the invention of many stories of extraterrestrial activity and submerged cities to explain the existence of the Moais. Although these theories have been ruled out, this vibrant culture will always remain somewhat of a mystery.

— Chapter Seven —

FOOD

DON'T ORDER CHILLI IN CHILE

As experienced expatriates, we know that food is one of the major components of culture shock. Three times a day, or perhaps even more, you are reminded that you are not in your homeland. Yet with any luck you will discover tasty Chilean delicacies which will be difficult to leave behind when your stay is over. Take advantage of your stay to collect Chilean recipes and try your hand at new and different meals. If your time in Chile is limited, try and focus your culinary arts on those recipes that do not require special ingredients.

SCHEDULE

Breakfast

The first meal of the day in Chile is *desayuno* or breakfast, which is generally eaten around 7:00 a.m. It is rather light fare – bread and jam with milk for the children and *café con leche* or tea for the adults is typical. *Café con leche* is half a cup of hot coffee with half a cup of hot milk, sweetened to taste with sugar. Energy drinks such as Milo are also common for children.

Lunch

Almuerzo or lunch is the big meal of the day in Chile, and it is generally eaten between 1:00 and 2:00 p.m. Traditionally, two main dishes are served at lunch. The first dish may be a salad of some kind. The second course is generally a more substantial meat dish with vegetables as accompaniment, although there are several Chilean vegetarian main dishes. In small towns and in some parts of big cities, businesses close from 1:00 to 3:00 p.m. so people can go home and have lunch with their families. Most businesses today in the larger cities stay open all day. Most Chilean schools do not serve lunch to students, so they arrive home very hungry. However, this will be changing with the implementation of educational reforms that call for a full-day schedule.

Once

The third meal of the day, *once*, is at 5:00 p.m. not 11:00 p.m. as the name implies. It is afternoon tea with bread and jam, sandwiches, pastries or a cake. It is very typical for children and adults alike to invite people over to share *once*.

There are at least three versions of how teatime got its name in Chile. The first version claims that it is named after the time that the British have their tea – 11:00 a.m. Another version claims that it is named after a variety of English biscuits called elevenses that the British served with their tea. The third version says that at teatime the men went to the kitchen or back room to have a sip of *aguardiente*, a grape spirit, instead of tea. However, the men didn't want to say that they were drinking liquor. Since the word *aguardiente* has 11 letters, they called it *once*.

Dinner

Dinner in Chile is referred to as *la comida* and not *cena* as in many other Spanish-speaking countries. Only in rural areas will you hear the word *cena*. Dinner is typically served at 8:30 p.m. if there are young children, or later if the children are older. Dinner is usually one main dish, which is generally interchangeable with those served as a main course for lunch. The meal is substantial and foreigners may find it too heavy to eat at such a late hour.

CHILEAN CUISINE

Main Courses

There is a common misperception that Chileans eat spicy food. Do not confuse the dishes of the Southern Cone with Mexican or Tex-Mex food. In general, the majority of Chilean meals are either hearty meat dishes or rich seafood dishes. *Ají*, a spicy condiment, is sometimes added, but mouth-burning meals are not the norm.

Special Dishes

Chileans have many main dishes where the principal ingredient is not meat or fish. One of the tastiest is *humitas*, made by grating fresh corn (*choclo*) and mixing it into a paste with fried onions, basil, salt, and pepper. The mixture is then wrapped in corn husks and dropped into boiling water to cook. The corn to make *humitas* is not typical corn found in most of the world; it is white, not yellow, and has huge individual kernels. (Laura has seen popcorn larger than a golf ball made from this white corn!) It is not sweet, and is perfect for baking. Try boiled *choclo* with butter and salt as the Chileans eat it.

Another typical Chilean main dish is *porotos granados*, a healthy combination of beans, squash and corn. Beans are called *porotos*, not *frijoles*, in Chile.

Pastel de choclo is another dish using white corn, this time in a corn and meat casserole topped with sugar. *Prieta* is a typical Chilean sausage filled with cabbage and blood! The name comes from the Portuguese word *preta* which means black. There are many hearty stews served as main courses. *Cazuela* has just about everything in it – meat, chicken, and/or seafood served in large chunks with a variety of vegetables and rice. *Curanto* is another stew typical of Chiloé. It can be made with almost anything – fish, shellfish, meat and/or vegetables – and then tossed together and cooked. It is traditionally cooked underground in a pit, but today it is sometimes cooked in pots.

Beef

For a country that has such a long coastline, it is interesting that beef remains so popular. It is generally of good quality, but most Chileans admit that Argentinean beef is superior. There are a number of restaurants in Chile that serve only *parrilladas*. A *parrillada* is a small barbeque brought to your table overflowing with assorted cuts of beef and sausages. Some foreigners are shocked by *parrillada*, which can include almost every part of the beast, including intestines, stomachs, hearts and other tasty treats. There are also typical Chilean blood sausages, so if this is not to your taste be sure to request the preferred cuts or ask what it is before you accept it on your plate.

Another characteristic beef dish is *bistec a lo pobre*, a steak topped with two fried eggs and served with french fries and fried onions. Although the name means "poor man's steak," Chileans joke that the name should be changed to *bistec a lo rico* (rich man's steak) since it is expensive. Do not confuse this typical meal with steak au poivre, which is a French pepper steak dish that is not common in Chile. *Carne mechada* is another popular dish. A thick piece of meat is tenderized in a vinegar marinade and cooked with carrots.

Seafood

As you can imagine, there is an incredible variety of seafood available in Chile. Typical seafood dishes include: sea barnacles (*choritos*), octopus (*pulpo*), sea urchin (*erizos*), ray (*raya*), seaweed (*cochayuyo*), *picorocos*, king crab (*centolla*), salmon, clams (*machas*), sea bass (*mero*), abalone (*locos*), flounder (*lenguado*), hake (*merluza*), smelt (*pejerrey*), trout (*trucha*), kingklip (*congrio*), corvina, oysters (*ostras*) and scallops (*ostiones*), just to name a few.

Seafood is prepared in many different ways. *Cebiche*, which is raw seafood mixed with lots of lemon juice, tomatoes, onions and spices, is one popular method. It is important to remember that *cebiche* is not cooked, and while the lemon juice pickles the seafood, it does not kill any bacteria. The popularity of *cebiche* in Peru was one of the main reasons for the high death toll in that country during an outbreak of cholera in the early 1990s. Although Chile was spared in

For fresh and exotic seafood in Santiago, visit the Mercado Central.

that outbreak due to rigid health controls, it should remind us that *cebiche* is only as good as the hygiene of the chef.

Selling abalone is illegal in Chile when it is out of season due to the depletion of its numbers. However, unscrupulous fishermen will still offer to sell it to you on the beaches. Recently the government has relaxed the restrictions as the abalone population is making a comeback.

Empanadas

There are literally hundreds of types of *empanadas* in South America. As the name implies, *empanadas* can be anything covered with a bread-like outer shell. Basically there are two categories of *empanadas* – baked and fried. What is inside is a regional speciality. A typical Chilean *empanada* is filled with a mixture of chopped beef, onion, olives, raisins, and hardboiled eggs and is called *empanada de pino*. *Empanadas* can also be filled with cheese and fried. The *empanada* called *pequén* is typically Chilean. Filled with onions, it was originally only eaten by the poor, who could not afford meat. Today it is eaten solely for its flavor. You might also want to try Chilean seafood *empanadas*. Despite their large size, *empanadas* are usually eaten as an appetizer.

Salads

For those *gringos* who expect iceberg lettuce with a variety of dressings every time the word salad is mentioned, Chile is a shock. Laura finds it consoling to remember that the word *ensalada* ("and salad" in English) has its roots in Latin, meaning "in salt." That is a pretty broad description, and such are salads in Chile. Generally, *ensaladas* in Chile are cold vegetables dressed with oil and lemon, and lettuce is not one of the more common ingredients. A very popular type is the *ensalada chilena* with chopped, peeled tomatoes and sliced onions dressed in salt, oil, vinegar, coriander and cilantro.

Breads

In many areas of Chile, the tradition of eating bread, bought fresh every morning from the local *panadería*, is still honored. Some bread sellers even deliver bread to their regular customers' homes every day, although this is becoming less common. Bread is sold by the kilo and is never refrigerated. Chileans would consider that an insult. *Chapalele* is a typical bread from Chiloé made from potatoes and wheat flour and boiled. *Milcao* is also made from potatoes and originated in Chiloé. *Sopaipilla* is an unbaked bread made from *zapallo* or Chilean pumpkin. It is sometimes served with a warm caramel sauce and together they are called *sopaipillas pasadas*. This is usually only eaten in winter when it is cold and rainy as they are supposed to warm you up!

Hallullas, *marraquetas* and *pan amasado* are the most popular varieties of bread found in Chile. *Hallullas* are round, flat pieces of white bread. The *marraqueta* is a small, dense, French type of white bread. Actually, most bread in Chile is somewhat dense. *Pan amasado*, a very traditional bread, is cooked without yeast and therefore is very flat and very dense. *Pan de molde*, sold in supermarkets, is somewhat fluffy, and is the closest thing to American sandwich bread. Chileans love white bread and it may be more difficult to find wheat or other multigrain breads. If you are looking for something to top your bread try *quesillo*, a light cheese with the consistency of tofu. It is very popular and is served frequently at breakfast and *once*.

Desserts

Chileans have a sweet tooth that is only satisfied by very sweet desserts. Even tea and juice are made with a great amount of sugar. Desserts at lunchtime generally consist of fruit accompanied by ice cream. If you want it without ice cream just order *compote*. An interesting dessert is *leche nevada*, where meringues are added to a sugary egg yolk and milk mixture, and then frozen. Many desserts

have a meringue component, including the various types of *suspiros*. Eggs are also the base for flan, a classic in all Spanish speaking countries. Another typical Chilean dessert is *platano en dulce*, bananas sprinkled with cornmeal, spices and powdered sugar and baked.

Fruits in Chile are generally eaten with a fork and knife, not with the fingers. For example, an apple is peeled, often in one long connected spiral, and then sliced and eaten with a fork. Actually, most foods are eaten with a knife and fork, including pizza, sandwiches, french fries, chicken, etc. Only some appetizers and snacks may be eaten with the fingers.

Many of the typical Chilean sweet bread toppings come in tin cans. *Dulce de membrillo* (sweet quince) is not too sweet and has the consistency of hardened jam. *Manjar blanco*, a.k.a. *dulce de leche*, is the bread topping of choice for much of Latin America. It also comes in tins, or plastic containers, and is basically cooked sweetened condensed milk. There is a way to make *manjar blanco* at home by cooking a can of sweetened condensed milk, but you should consult a good recipe book or a Chilean friend before attempting it. *Manjar* is spread on bread like peanut butter or Nutella, and the large containers available at the supermarkets testify to the fact that it is extremely popular. It turns up in countless cakes and sweets, such as *panqueque celestino*, crepes, *torta mil hojas* and *manjar relleno* – a sweet donut-like fried pastry into which warm *manjar* is poured.

Picarones are Chilean donuts and they also come in a *pasados* version with the caramel sauce. *Calzones rotos* (yes, "torn under-wear!") are strips of dough with a hole sliced in the middle and one end is pulled through to give it a twisty shape. Then of course there is Spanish *churros*, a long, round, fried pastry sprinkled with sugar and cinnamon. On many street corners you will find hawkers selling *cuchuflí*, small tube-like cookies filled with *manjar*.

While at the supermarket do not pass up the varieties of refrigerated prepared desserts sold in plastic cups. Nestlé is very big in Chile and all of South America, and does a good job of providing tasty, inexpensive desserts. Europeans may be more familiar with these and other prepared foods available in Chile. For many, they are a welcome addition to the refrigerator.

ALCOHOLIC BEVERAGES

One of the first things that people associate with Chile is its wine. The central region of the country has an ideal climate for producing wine – warm summers, rain-free autumns, moderate winters, and a mild spring with no frosts to kill young vines. Critics liken Chilean wines to French wines rather than Californian wines for flavor. Wines are graded according to quality – *gran vino* (good), *vino especial* (better), and *vino reservado* (excellent). It is worthwhile to become somewhat versed in Chilean wines.

It may come as a shock to parents to find out that their teens have relatively easy access to alcohol. It is inevitable that some foreign teens go wild, at least for a while. After a few unpleasant episodes, most teens follow the Chilean example and drink responsibly.

Pisco is a transparent spirit similar to brandy. It is produced in the Elqui Valley where the climate is hot, with 300 days a year of clear skies, low rainfall and very little wind. The grapes grown here have a very high sugar content. *Pisco* is popular for mixing with soft drinks like Coca Cola (called *piscola*), ginger ale or vermouth but it is most common in Pisco sour. This classic drink is made with lemon juice, sugar, ice and beaten egg white. The Peruvians made this drink famous, but the Chilean version tastes slightly different.

Vaina is a tasty mixture of port wine with egg white and cinnamon. *Aguardiente* "fire water" is very strong, and is also made from distilled grapes. It is often served around Christmas in *cola de mono*. *Chicha*, borrowed from the Amerindians, is made from fermented grapes. It tastes like apple cider and is popular on National Day.

Toasts

Chileans always toast after the first drink has been poured, and before anyone has taken a sip. It is usually a few words in honor of the host, or in honor of the occasion. All glasses are raised and everyone says "Salud" (health) in unison. After the initial toast, there may be random "Saluds" throughout the evening. Eye contact is usually made with those around the table while the glass is raised.

OTHER BEVERAGES

Non-alcoholic beverages are also popular in Chile. Fruit juices made in blenders are common. They are made with either milk or water and may contain added sugar, so be sure to specify. Soda is consumed in vast amounts in Chile. Most meals are accompanied by juice or soda (*bebidas*) and if you request just plain water, most will not believe you. For the average Chilean *bebidas* are far superior to a glass of plain water.

Yerba mate is very popular in the Southern Cone – Argentina, Chile, Paraguay and Uruguay. It is a ground herb that is set to steep in a cup or gourd and sipped through a metal straw that strains the herb. After supper some Chileans have *mate*, particularly in the south, as it is supposed to be good for digestion. There are many herbal teas to sample in Chile and they are referred to as *aguitas*. They include herbs found in Chile such as *boldo*, *rosa mosqueta*, *cedrón* and *paico*. *Manzanilla* (chamomile) tea is popular.

RESTAURANTS

You may think that an Italian restaurant would be the same in London, Miami or Santiago, but that would only be true if all the people who worked there were Italian and if all the ingredients were bought in Italy. Chileans have their own idea of how a restaurant should be run. The waiters come right away to ask for your order, but prompt follow-up service after the food has been served is rare, which foreigners tend to think of as bad service. Chileans, on the other hand, would think this was intruding. You are not given much time to consider the options, but then again there are generally not many options. Almost all typical Chilean restaurants have the same basic menu. You have to ask for the check, as Chileans reserve the right to linger over coffee for hours, and bringing the check immediately after finishing would imply that you should leave.

Water is not automatically served in Chilean restaurants, but spicy *ají* is sometimes on the table. *Ají* is eaten as a spice on most foods. *Pebre*, also found on the table, is a mixture of tomatoes, onions, cilantro, oil and a little chilli that many eat with bread. It may come as a shock that you must pay extra for lettuce, tomato, mayonnaise, vegetables, potatoes (which are almost never baked in Chile) or extra rolls, etc., to accompany the meal. Note that you must be careful when ordering coffee, as "*café*" will come as Nescafé instant coffee. If you want brewed coffee ask for "*café café*." In Chile the tip is not included in the bill, and 10% is normal.

As the country has become wealthier, dining out has become very popular in recent years. In addition to the large number of Chilean restaurants there is a multitude of fast food chain restaurants, both Chilean and foreign. The first Chilean chain was lomito'n, which serves sandwiches and has pictures on the menu to help you decide (or order, if your Spanish is not so good). Chileans do not share tables at restaurants and even at fast food restaurants they would prefer to sit alone.

If you tire of Chilean food, there are many other foreign restaurants to choose from, at least in Santiago. Spanish, Argentinean, Mexican, Italian, Peruvian, German, Chinese and even more exotic

Lomito'n was the first Chilean restaurant chain and is a good option for a quick meal.

restaurants are opening as the country becomes more sophisticated and affluent. However, these restaurants can be expensive.

Café Haití is a chain of coffee houses that has become a Chilean institution. Concentrated in downtown Santiago, patrons, predominantly men, stand at the counter and drink coffee. The trick is that the waitresses are dressed in the tightest and shortest dresses you've ever seen. This gimmick has spawned imitators. Recently new coffee houses have opened where the women wear sleazy lingerie. There is even one aimed at female patrons where the waiters (all male) wear only tight leather shorts.

GROCERY STORES

In cities of any considerable size in Chile, supermarkets are well-stocked, and often cheaper than the open-air street *ferias*. Imported goods are available at many supermarkets in limited amounts. Jumbo, a "hypermarket," has the largest selection of imported items, with many products from the United States and Europe, especially Germany. Milk is generally whole in Chile, but skim is available. There is an ample variety of diet sodas.

At the entrance to the supermarket you will notice a large bottle return section. Most beer and carbonated beverages come in glass or heavy plastic bottles marked "*retornable*," for which you will be required to pay a small deposit. You are entitled to the deposit when returning the bottle, but most people use the credit towards another bottle. You will be given a slip of paper with the number of bottles which should be given to the cashier. Otherwise you will be charged an additional deposit. In small neighborhood stores, just return the bottles when you buy more, no slip will be issued.

Generally, a young boy or girl will bag your groceries. He or she may not be an employee of the store, so it is correct to give a tip for the service, even if you did not request it. While at the check-out, make sure that you get all your items, as sometimes there is confusion as to which items belong to whom.

117

If you want local color not available in a supermarket, head to the Mercado Central. Located in downtown Santiago, it is the place to go for fresh seafood. The building's architecture was inspired by Eiffel. It is very old with small booths where the stall owners can even cook the food right there for you. For fresh produce, many people in Santiago go to La Vega Central located near the Mapocho River. Groceries, produce and fresh flowers are sold wholesale and retail. On weekends, *ferias* or fruit and vegetable markets are set up in most neighborhoods. Produce fresh from the countryside is sold and it is well worth the extra stop.

In season, fruit and vegetables are cheap and very flavorful. You must remember to weigh your fruit and vegetables in the supermarkets in the special weighing section, not at the check-out. All vegetables and fruit should be washed in disinfectant solution that can be bought in the supermarkets because of the heavy use of pesticides. Some water in Chile contains levels of bacteria that may upset the foreigner's stomach, especially upon arrival. Chileans may swear that your water is safe, but they may be immune to the problem.

Many foreigners, however, do drink tap water without incident. Just remember that juice and ice in Chile are both made with tap water, so choose which you are most comfortable with.

Chapter Eight

LANGUAGE

SPANISH, CHILEAN STYLE

The official language of Chile is Spanish, the language brought by the conquistadors several hundred years ago. Despite the time and distance, Spanish spoken in Latin America is remarkably similar to Spanish spoken in Spain. There are many more pronunciation and vocabulary differences between the English spoken in the US and England. All Spanish speakers can communicate with one another quite easily. Chilean Spanish has a few local words borrowed from its Indian groups, which make it unique.

One of the first surprises in Chile is that children do not learn Spanish in school, but rather *castellano*. The terms "*español*" and "*castellano*" are equivalents in describing the language of Chile, but *castellano* is used more frequently. It does not refer to any language specific to the Castile region of Spain (near Toledo), as the name implies, rather it is a derivation of the word for the Spanish language that pays homage to the historic importance of the kingdom of Castile in the formation of the modern Spanish state. So don't worry that you may learn some deviant type of Spanish in Chile. Throughout South America, *"castellano"* is the word used for Spanish. *"Español"* is more common in Central and North America.

PRONUNCIATION

Regional differences in the language of the Chilean people are remarkably slight, despite the country's varied geography and great length. Chilean Spanish is generally the same from north to south, a result of the fact that the Spaniards settled in a small area in the center of the country and migrated slowly and in small numbers to the north and the south. Today, television and radio help to homogenize Chilean Spanish.

There are, however, noticeable differences in accents, usually based on socio-economic background. As in most countries, the upper classes and the educated speak a more refined language than the lower classes.

As far as pronunciation goes, Chilean Spanish does not have any colossal variations from other Latin American Spanish, only slight modifications that make Chilean sound Chilean. The pronunciations listed below are common in popular Chilean Spanish and in the informal speech of educated speakers:

The "d" is lost in the endings -ado and -ido: hablao (*hablado*)

The "d" is almost lost in the endings -ad and -ud: verdá (*verdad*), salú (*salud*).

The intervocalic "d" is almost lost: deo (*dedo*), náa (*nada*).

The intervocalic "r" is weak: páa (*para*).

The omission of the intervocalic "g" is considered vulgar: juar (*jugar*).

Simple pleasures like buying ice cream will require some knowledge of Spanish.

The "s" may be pronounced completely (*asno*), aspirated (*ahno*), assimilated (*anno*), or completely omitted (*fóforo*). The "ch" may be more fricative, or similar to the "sh" sound. For example: Shile, Pinoshet. However, this is considered to be a sign of a lack of culture. Chileans tend to put in a rolled "r" sound before certain words that they would like to emphasize – "Rrrrrr – Qué bueno."

A large part of what gives foreigners that *extranjero* sound in Spanish is the pronunciation of a sentence. The individual words are often pronounced well, but that is precisely the error. It is the nature of Spanish to start every syllable with a consonant, thereby frequently linking one word with the next. For example, "Los amigos aman a las Ariqueñas" will be pronounced in everyday speech like this: "Lo sa mi go sa ma na la sa ri que ñas." Listen to Chileans in natural conversation to get a feel for this.

Our best advice on picking up a good accent is to study intently the lips and tongue position and to imitate it. It takes training to make your mouth take these shapes. An English accent in Chile has been compared to talking with a hot potato in one's mouth. Laura remembers that her mouth ached when she started to learn Spanish in earnest. But realistically, anyone who learns a language after puberty will have some trace of an accent.

VOCABULARY

One must be very careful when imitating the colloquial vocabulary in any country. Native speakers have much more leeway when it comes to using popular speech, which often sounds silly or insulting coming from foreigners. This applies especially to vulgar words. It is easy to pick up bad words, not always knowing what they mean literally, but knowing when they are used. It is best to try to find more elegant terminology to express your sentiments.

Be sure to ask the Chileans about their slang and pronunciations, as they love to explain them to visitors. The following is a small list of the highlights of Chilean slang:

Ahuasado – naive or a shy person (comes from *huaso* – a country bumpkin or cowboy). This is somewhat of an insult to *huasos*, even though the term "*huaso*" itself has no negative connotation

Al tiro – quickly

Bachichas – Italians

Beatle – turtleneck (in deference to the Fab Four)

Cabros – kids

¿*Cachai?* – "Get it?" added to the end of many sentences

Cacharro – auto

Cachureo – junk, things of low value

Cartera – purse (not wallet as in other Spanish-speaking countries)

Coños – Spaniards, called so because of how often the Spanish use this expletive

Cuico/a – a conservative person, generally of a socio-economic class above one's own, a snob, someone who flaunts his/her wealth

Chaleco – cardigan or vest

Ches – Argentineans

Cholos – Peruvians or Bolivians, also a degrading term for Indians

Choro – an exclamation similar to "cool!"

Chomba or *chompa* – sweater

Chupamedias or *patero* – someone who sucks up to his/her boss

Darse vuelta la chaqueta – to change political affiliation

Dije – nice

Falluto or *chueco* – one who is not always correct

Fome – boring

Gabachos – French

Gringos – Americans and Britons

Gordo/a – term of endearment, literally fat or fatty

Guagua – baby

Harto – 1) adjective – a lot, plenty; 2) verb – *estar harto/a* – to be fed up, unable to stand or support something anymore

Huevón/ona n.& adj. – can be a vulgar expression or an affectionate chiding. To say this while holding one hand palm up, fingers curled, as if holding an apple, is a very obscene and insulting gesture.

Lolo/a – teenager

Luca – 1,000 (commonly used to refer to 1,000 pesos)

Negro/a – a term of endearment

Onda – the essence or spirit of something, often used in the expression *¿Qué onda?* – What's up? or What's your problem?

¡Oye! – an informal greeting, roughly the equivalent of "hey," but much more widespread

Pacos – police officers

Patrona – wife, which shows who has the power in the Chilean family!

Pega – work

Pelados – members of the army (because of their short haircuts), also a term of endearment for babies

Pelusas – poor children

Pesado/a – an obnoxious person or a party pooper

Pinchar – to win someone over, or score (i.e. with a woman or man)

Pico – although this word is widely used in many other countries, meaning a little, in Chile it is slang for penis

Pituto – a contact who can arrange for special treatment or privileges

¡Plop! – an interjection which expresses surprise or bewilderment, taken from the Chilean comic strip *Condorito*

Polera – T-shirt

Pololear – to go steady, to have a serious romantic relationship with someone

Pololo/a – boyfriend/girlfriend

Por si acaso – just in case or by the way

Pu or *Po* – an abbreviated form of *pues*, used to add emphasis, generally at the end of a sentence. e.g. *¡Si po! ¡No po!*

Rasca – in bad taste, tacky, of bad quality or poorly made; or a low-class person or someone without manners

Regalón/ona – the pet or favorite person, one that is spoiled or pampered

Regalonear – to pamper

Regio – super, great, excellent

Rico – excellent, good, referring to food or drink, or an attractive, sexy person

Roto or *picante* – an unrefined person

Salvaje – an upper-class (*cuico*) term meaning great

Si po' – an abbreviated form of *Si pues*, yes or of course

Sinvergüenza – a person who is unafraid to say what he/she thinks; a crook

Suche – lowly worker

Taco – traffic jam or the heel of a shoe

¿Te fijas? – Get it? Did you understand?

Tintolio – red wine

Tucada – salary or a great sum of money

OTHER LANGUAGE CONSIDERATIONS

Voseo

If you have studied Spanish formally, you may remember the informal second person plural form is *vosotros*. We say "may" because many textbooks omit the form completely, since, for the most part, it is not used by the great majority of Spanish speakers. In Chile *voseo* may be considered a sign of poor education. While the textbooks claim it is the second person plural, most people use it as the informal singular, in other words, replacing the *tú* form with the *vosotros* form. For example *¿Cómo estáis?* or the abbreviated *¿Cómo estái?* is a common expression when talking to one person, when theoretically it should be used for more than one person.

You may also hear people substitute the subject pronoun *vos* for *tú*, another phenomenon common throughout Latin America. Do note that even though the speaker uses the subject pronoun *vos*, the indirect and direct object pronoun is still *te* and the possessive forms are still *tu* and *tuyo*. For example, *¡Vos quédate aquí!*, *¿Vas vos en tu auto?* However, substituting *vos* for *tú* in Chile is a sign of poor education, unlike in other Latin American countries where its use is widespread.

Tú versus Usted

One aspect of the Spanish language that makes it different from the English language is the division of pronouns into formal or informal. Every person you speak with must be classified into one or the other category. This is a tough call for many foreigners in Chile, especially native English speakers, who are unused to making the distinction. Many people have the mistaken notion that it would be better to use the informal term with everyone, but this is not the true nature of the Spanish language. In general, native speakers probably use *Usted* much more than *tú* once they leave their houses. Unless you marry a Chilean or have many intimate friends, the formal form will be much more important to you.

Usted is actually an abbreviation of *Vuestra Merced*, roughly translated as "Your Grace," a title used in Spain hundreds of years ago. It is important to remember that *Usted* is the norm and *tú* is a privilege only granted to certain individuals. *Usted* is used with guests, older people, anyone in a position of authority, or anyone you do not know. *Usted* is always used in business relationships, even if the social status is the same. You may have known your secretary, boss or colleague for many years, but the relationship will always be on an *Usted* basis. Even among family members *Usted* can be heard, especially with distant relatives, when there is a large age gap between family members, or with relatives by marriage. Some parents use the *Usted* form with their children as a term of endearment.

With people of your own age and status whom you meet in a social setting you will probably start off using *tú*. It is recommended that you follow the lead of Chileans until you are able to judge for yourself. The change from *Usted* to *tú* can happen quickly, and marks the recognition of a certain intimacy in the relationship.

In some cases one person may use *Usted*, while the other uses *tú*. This may happen when adults speak to children (or between any two people with a large age gap – be careful not to offend an older person by using *tú* with them in response to their use of *tú* with you!), or when servants speak to employers and vice versa. To use a famous example, Don Quixote used *tú* when speaking with Sancho Panza, his manservant, but Sancho always used *Vuestra Merced* with Don Quixote, his master. This example is of course from 17th century Spanish literature, but the principle is still valid in Chile today.

The term *"Don"* comes from the phrase *De Origen Noble* (of noble origin). It replaces the title *Señor*. Today in Chile the terms *"Don"* and *"Doña"* (for women) are used to show respect. They are

often used to show extreme respect when addressing someone with a remarkably important position, such as ambassador, minister or other high offices. It would be perfectly acceptable to address President Frei as Don Eduardo. It is also used to show respect even if social status is not that different. *Empleadas* and *nanas* always address their male employers as *Don* and female employers as *Doña* or *Señora*. If the *empleada* is older, she will, in turn, be addressed as *Doña* or *Señora*. An office worker may use *Don* to address a boss. Similarly, the junior (a male employee responsible for miscellaneous errands), although from a lower social standing, will be addressed as *Don* if he is older. Use of the term is linked to the use of *Usted*. No matter how close these relationships become, as a sign of respect, the informal *tú* will never be used. Chileans, no matter what their social level, would never refer to themselves as *Don* or *Doña*, as this would seem presumptuous.

Chapter Nine

SOCIAL AND BUSINESS CUSTOMS

MAKING A CONNECTION

Chilean society is, for the most part, very warm and welcoming. Whether you are in a social or business situation, the rules of conduct are basically the same – a connection needs to be made on a personal level. It is easy to establish a personal rapport with acquaintances or colleagues merely by being friendly and showing an interest in their families and the country. Because of its importance in Chilean society, common courtesy dictates that a person's family be one of the first topics of discussion. Furthermore, in Chile, as in many other places, a willingness to learn about the country and its people will start you off on the right foot.

The best way to impress business associates is to invite them to your home to meet your family.

RELATIONS WITH FOREIGNERS

It is precisely this emphasis on family that has prevented some foreigners from breaking into Chilean culture. Chileans believe that if you are with your family, your central needs are being met and therefore there is no need to take you under their wing. Chileans show much more concern for a person who is alone, and therefore extend more invitations to those without family. This sentiment is expressed by many Chileans who describe themselves as *"abandonado y triste"* (abandoned and sad) when a spouse is away on business or holiday.

There is a genuine interest and an overall positive attitude towards foreigners in Chile. In certain Latin American countries, Americans in general are not well-liked and may be treated with animosity. In Chile, however, this is definitely not the case. Reactions can be either positive or neutral, but will seldom be outright hostile.

All North American and European foreigners are called *gringos*, but this should not be taken as an insult. Sometimes, it is used as a term of endearment, i.e., *la gringita*. The United States is often jokingly referred to as *Gringolandia*.

VISITING A CHILEAN HOME

One of the most common ways Chileans express their hospitality is to invite you into their homes. If you are invited *a comer* or to *una comida* this should be translated as dinner. The more formal word *cena* is not regularly used except by those who live in southern Chile. The dinner hour is very late in Chile, beginning no earlier than 9:00 p.m. and sometimes as late as 10:30 p.m. If you have not yet adapted to the Chilean eating schedule you may want to snack beforehand, although hors d'oeuvres most likely will be offered. The dinner may be the focus of the evening, but it by no means suggests the end. Conversation continues long afterward, so expect a late night.

Be Polite, Arrive Late!

Latin Americans are notorious for arriving late to almost any event. In Chile this holds true for social events, but not for business meetings. Even though you may consider it rude behavior in your country, it would in fact be rude to show up to a party or a dinner at the time indicated. If the hosts invite you for dinner at 8:00 p.m., they will not expect you before 8:20. If you do arrive at the time indicated, the hosts may be shocked to see you. Laura was once greeted by a hostess in her bathrobe and curlers when she arrived "on time."

Attire

Chileans tend to dress up for all manner of social events (with the exception of picnics). Even if you have been invited to an "informal" dinner, the Chilean guests will be dressed quite formally. Some younger Chileans may wear fashionable casual wear, but they will seldom don blue jeans or shorts.

Gifts

It is customary to bring a small gift to the hostess to show your appreciation for her hospitality and for dinner (even if she has a maid).

Appropriate gifts are chocolates, a bottle of wine, flowers, etc. Fruit baskets are not common in Chile, maybe because fruit is extremely cheap. If the family has small children, you could bring them toys, but this is definitely not required.

You may also be invited to an *asado* over the weekend or on a holiday. An *asado* is an outdoor barbeque either in someone's backyard or in a park. The main focus of the meal is meat, lots of meat, but a few side salads and bread will also be served. Only if you have been specifically asked will you be expected to bring a portion of the meal. The same small gifts mentioned above can be given to the hostess. If you happen to be invited to *once* (afternoon tea), it would be appropriate to bring pastries, sweets or even a cake if there are many people.

GREETINGS

When greeting or taking their leave of each other most Chilean women will kiss each other once on the right cheek. Men and women do the same when arriving or leaving. Men shake hands, although close friends may shake hands and embrace. These greetings are common only in social situations and may not be appropriate in business settings depending upon the relationship. If there is a large number of people, Chileans will still make the rounds greeting everyone individually. Only when attending a very large party will you be exempt from doing so.

When you are ready to leave mention that you must be going, but do not jump up and bolt out the door. The first time you state your intention it is merely a warning that you will be leaving soon. Conversation should continue for about 10 to 15 minutes longer. After such time, you can stand up, state that you must be going and ask for your coat. You may, however, find it difficult to disengage yourself from the conversation. There is a running joke in Chile that friends continue to chat even after the car has pulled away and is

Close friends greet each other with an abrazo.

driving down the street. If you have your own car, it would be appropriate and greatly appreciated if you offered a ride to anyone without one, regardless of whether it is on your way home or not. If you do not have a way home, don't be surprised if someone you just met offers you a ride. This is part of Chilean hospitality.

Conversation

In general, conversations at dinners and parties in Chile are not that different from those in many other countries. Conversation will usually begin with your family, i.e., children, siblings, parents, etc. and their occupations. You should show similar interest in the families of the hosts and other guests. People will also be curious as to why you are in Chile, your profession and where and what you studied. Naturally they will be interested in your impressions of their country and whether you've had a chance to travel. Chileans are very proud and will wholeheartedly agree with compliments you make

133

regarding the economic progress and physical beauty of the country. You may find Chileans more critical of other aspects of life in Chile, however, and they will be interested to know how life in Chile compares to life in your home country. Although very proud, Chileans tend to be self-deprecating, often making jokes about what a backward country Chile is or how dishonest their fellow Chileans are. You are not expected to agree with these claims wholeheartedly.

Chileans are not generally concerned with keeping the conversation "politically correct." When speaking about other groups of people, whether from different cultures or different sexual orientation, some conversations may appear harsh, insensitive and derogatory. Most Chileans firmly believe that they are not racists, yet this assertion has rarely been tested as many have never been exposed to other nationalities. There is also a tendency for some Chileans to look down on indigenous groups within the country. This attitude lingers in spite of the higher standing these groups have achieved as part of an overall growing interest in environmental and indigenous issues, particularly among the younger generation. The terms *indio* and *cholo* in reference to the native population carry negative connotations, and although they are commonly used, we would suggest that you refrain from including them in your vocabulary.

Another topic often introduced is body weight. It is not considered rude to remark on someone's weight gain or loss. It is not meant as an insult, merely an observation. In fact, this is true with many other physical attributes, for example, hairstyles. If you are unfortunate enough to get a really bad haircut, no one will lie to make you feel better. A friend was once asked if someone had cut his hair with an ax. Although he understood Chilean culture quite well and knew it was not meant as an insult, he was nevertheless hurt by her candid remarks. The same Chilean also told him that a friend of his was quite ugly. The best advice is to just ignore the comment because there is no malice intended. On the other hand, you'll know that a compliment is heartfelt and not meant to make you feel better. Chileans can also be equally blunt about your Spanish-speaking capabilities, although they will continuously encourage you to practice and are more than willing to help. Chileans are flattered when a foreigner attempts to learn Spanish and they often excitedly explain the intricacies of Chilean slang.

It is not acceptable to discuss salaries unless you are among very close friends. It is fine to ask how much an impersonal item cost, such as a major appliance, but you should refrain from asking about the cost of more personal items such as jewelry. Chileans are more relaxed when discussing rent.

RUDE BEHAVIOR

Always cover your mouth while yawning. Holding your hand palm up, fingers curled as if you're holding an apple is an extremely insulting and obscene gesture. Chewing gum is not appropriate in a formal situation. Hats should never be worn indoors and it is rude to walk around barefoot inside someone's home. According to superstition, a woman should never set her purse on the floor as this will cause her to lose money.

Do not expect to watch television when visiting Chileans in their home. Upon entering the living room you may be struck by the feeling that something is missing. In most Chilean homes, televisions are in the bedrooms. Living rooms are for visiting only. If you become close friends with someone, you may be invited into the bedroom to watch television. This invitation, in most instances, is perfectly innocent and should not be misconstrued.

Don't Look the Other Way

On the surface, Chileans may appear to be more outgoing than perhaps your fellow countrymen. Once you have met someone, they will go out of their way to greet you if you happen upon each other on the street or at another function. We know of many Americans who have pretended not to notice someone for fear of becoming involved in a long-drawn-out conversation. Chileans, like all Latinos, do just the opposite and will track you down to say hello and ask how you are doing, even if it is just for a second. Susan once was sitting in a running car waiting to pick up her husband when a friend walked by. Instead of just waving, he walked all the way around the car just to greet her with a kiss on the cheek and say hello. It can be time-consuming, but it is a very nice gesture that makes you feel well-liked, respected and appreciated. If you run into someone you know, you'd be better off in the long run stopping and chatting than being caught trying to avoid recognition.

A NIGHT OUT

It is not entirely uncommon to be invited out to dinner at a restaurant instead of someone's home. The issue of who pays the bill should be clear by the nature of the invitation. If the invitation is casual, most likely everyone will pay for themselves. Chileans will not squabble over exact amounts, so bills are split evenly. If you order only a soup to try and save money, your plan may not work. A foreigner being invited out for the first time will often be treated to dinner. Also, a single woman will never be expected to pay.

If you invite Chilean friends or colleagues over for dinner or out to a restaurant and they decline, you might find their excuse somewhat questionable. Do not worry that they don't like you or were trying to find a way out of spending an evening with you. They most likely have a very legitimate reason for not attending, but in their minds, it is better to tell a few half-truths than to be honest.

SMOKING

Chileans are heavy smokers, especially the women. Smoking is allowed in almost all public places. If you come from a country with stringent no-smoking policies, your lungs will have to adjust. Many people smoke in offices and restaurants (which are not divided into smoking and non-smoking sections) and do not feel uncomfortable lighting up in someone else's home. Yet, if you specifically ask them to refrain from smoking in your home they will honor your request and smoke outside or on the terrace.

TRANSACTING BUSINESS

In this section we will assume that those who are going to Chile for professional reasons already have a job, either with a multinational corporation (MNC) or with a Chilean firm. For those who do not have a specific job but would like to work in Chile it is always risky to arrive in a country without any concrete leads. It is not impossible for a foreigner to find work in Chile in a corporation or non-governmental organization, but it will take a lot of dedication and a little luck. If you have any *pitutos* (connections) your search may prove more fruitful. Many Americans who set off to Chile in search of work end up as private English teachers and, although financially this line of work is viable, professionally it may not be the best alternative for you. If you cannot find a job, you will be unable to secure a visa to stay in Chile on a long-term basis and will have to exit every three months.

General Business Climate

Chile's economy is open, the level of state intervention is minimal and free enterprise is strongly encouraged. The Chilean government is making every effort to attract foreign capital. In order to aid foreign investors, many government publications are available detailing start-up requirements, special trade zones, accounting requirements, corporate taxes, exchange rates, etc.

During the 1960s and 1970s, MNCs held considerable power in the Chilean economy. As a result, many Chileans greatly resented these companies and the people who represented them. Today, however, international companies are no longer seen as vehicles for robbing industrializing countries of their natural resources; they are now considered partners in development. Of course, some negative perceptions persist in a few sectors of society. For example, few Chileans would like to see the copper industry back in the hands of foreign companies, if only for nationalistic reasons. Furthermore, the environmental movement has a somewhat negative opinion of international companies. Some Chileans allege that these corporations, having destroyed their own homelands, are now pillaging the lands of the Third World.

The following section focuses on the general office environment in Chile. However, many people who have been posted to Chile will not find themselves behind a desk, especially those working in the mining, fishing and forestry industries. All in all, those who work in these fields may find a more relaxed working atmosphere. Moreover, in industries which have high levels of foreign investment, you may be working with Chileans who have had much more direct experience with foreigners. Each industry is unique, however, and because foreigners are involved in widely differing sectors from finance to hospitality to infrastructure, this section can provide only sweeping generalizations.

CULTURAL DIFFERENCES

In general, those who work in a branch office of a multinational corporation will encounter an overall work ethic close to that of the parent country. Nevertheless, when dealing with Chileans, either as clients or employees, even minor cultural differences must be taken into consideration. The most obvious differences are summarized below.

Business Meetings

Chileans tend to conduct their business affairs in the office. Unlike in many other countries where a major business deal is hammered out over an extended lunch, on the golf course or at a nightclub, Chileans close the deal in a formal business setting. It is very important to reconfirm any meeting or appointment close to the actual date.

Most offices have more than one telephone number. This is a holdover from the days when it was cheaper to add another line than to install a switchboard. Calling any of the numbers listed will put you in contact with the receptionist. It is also common practice in Chile for the secretary to screen and place most of her boss's calls. In the past, callers were attended to rather quickly, but today, with the sharp increase in business activity, people tend to be left on hold more often and for longer periods of time.

Punctuality should be observed in all business matters. Most business meetings begin with a handshake, regardless of the gender of those involved, especially if you are meeting for the first time. If the business relationship borders on a friendship, the greetings may be more demonstrative. Close associates may kiss each other on the cheek (if one is a woman) or they may embrace (if both are men).

To rush right into the topic of the meeting would be considered brash and rude. Business is conducted between two people, not between two firms, and as such a personal relationship needs to be developed. Chileans will always inquire about your family. This is not considered prying, but rather a friendly sign that they are truly interested. You should always ask about their families as well.

If time is not a problem, it would be a good idea to briefly bring up other topics like Chilean wines, the salmon industry, the pension system or the economy in general before getting to the heart of the matter. It shows that you have taken the time to learn about Chile and also gives Chileans an opportunity to boast about how well their country is doing.

In keeping with the Chilean belief that plain is better and fancy is in bad taste, business cards should be kept very simple. Name, title, firm and contact information should be written in plain script. Do not attempt to dress it up with colors, emblems or ornate logos.

Latin America is synonymous with graft for many people. This stereotype may have some basis in other countries, but in reality Chileans are remarkably honest. Grafting on all levels is considered a serious offense in Chile. In your business dealings with Chilean public officials you should be very careful not to imply that graft is a bargaining tool.

Guía Silber

The Guía Silber is a must for anyone wishing to do business in Chile. For those who are in Chile looking for work, it is the best place to begin. The Guía Silber is a comprehensive list providing the address and contact numbers of all government agencies, corporations, universities, non-governmental organizations, political parties, etc. However, it is not for sale in any bookstore. It must be purchased directly from the publisher, Silber Editores. The phone numbers in Santiago are 235-0814 or 235-0661 and the fax number is 235-0662. Their e-mail address is silber@mailnet.rdc.cl. The Publiguias publishing house produces good business reference guides (including the Yellow Pages or Paginas Amarillas). DECOM, a service found on the Internet, provides good business and legal information. You must pay a fee to access this website. In general, the Internet is a growing source of valuable information. Overall, reference material in Chile is good and up to date.

THE OFFICE ENVIRONMENT

Most likely you will experience some subtle differences between the Chilean workplace and the one to which you are accustomed. One major distinction is that the concept of "I'll get right on it" does not exist in Chile. If you ask someone to do a specific task, do not expect them to drop what they are doing to attend to your request. Regardless of the importance of the request, the Chilean will most likely say, "Yes, okay," which means "Just leave it with me and I'll get it done by the deadline." It will get done, but most things are done at the last minute, some only with prodding by nervous co-workers or bosses.

A recent study by the International Labor Organization found that Chile has the highest number of working hours per year of any country surveyed. On average, Chileans work 2,400 hours a year, more than their counterparts in Korea and Malaysia. This, however, does not translate into higher productivity.

Chile was low on the list of the World Competitiveness Report. The Chilean Undersecretary of Labor blamed it on the fact that Chileans tend to put things off, meaning they have to stay later at the office or go in on Saturdays. He also thought that Chileans do not work well in groups, or administer their time wisely. Of course, these are generalizations and, as in any culture, there are all types of workers. Moreover, it is important to remember that although Chileans are not as organized and productive as they potentially could be, the economy is, in fact, doing very well.

When Chileans work in groups on a specific project there is a tendency for one or two leaders to emerge. These leaders rise up to take responsibility and become much more involved in the project. As a result, they work much harder than the rest, who tend to lay back and let the others take control. Therefore, if questions or concerns arise, these members of the group appear to be "passing the buck" instead of dealing with them head-on. It is important to determine which employees are actively involved in a specific project.

The ability to speak Spanish is a very important tool for anyone working in Chile. Most educated Chileans can read English and many can understand English, but not all are fluent. Thus, being able to speak and understand Spanish will not only impress your colleagues, but will help you to do your job well.

Generally, office hours are from 8:30 a.m. or 9:00 a.m. to 5:30 p.m. or 6:00 p.m. from Monday to Friday. Banks are open Monday to Friday from 9:00 a.m. to 2:00 p.m. Government offices are open Monday to Friday, from 9:00 a.m. to 6:00 p.m., although some of them are open to the public only for limited periods during the day. Some offices may stay open even later depending on the work load. Chileans take a long lunch (one to two hours, although technically the lunch break should only be one hour). Most people in the major urban areas do not go home or take a *siesta*.

In some countries employees will only do what is specifically outlined in their job description. In Chile, the atmosphere is much more relaxed and a Chilean employee will be more likely to take on any number of tasks when asked. Similarly, Chileans work late when required, are loyal to the company and expect loyalty in return.

Although many offices may appear to operate very informally, do not be deceived. There is a clear hierarchy within the office no matter how democratically it seems to function. As explained in the language chapter, the formal version of the word you (*Usted*) is used in many cases. Furthermore, there are distinct class divisions among the office workers. Even though a secretary may be on very good terms with her boss, it is highly unlikely that they would associate outside of the office.

This up and coming business district in Santiago is often referred to as Sanhattan.

Attire

Office attire may be more formal in Chile than in your home nation. Smart dressing is the norm. For the most part, there are no "Dress down Fridays." Short-sleeved dress shirts are acceptable in warm weather and sweater vests are often worn during the cold winter months. Men always wear a jacket and tie for business, with navy being the predominant color. Men put on their jackets when leaving the office, even just for lunch. Women dress conservatively, mainly in dresses, skirts or suits. Most secretaries and clerks in large firms such as banks and government agencies wear uniforms. This is particularly helpful to women from lower income families who do not have the money to spend on work clothes.

Employees

When hiring local workers in Chile, you may be surprised to find their high school listed on the curriculum vitae in addition to the university. Chileans have the habit of writing extremely long resumés over-loaded with detailed information. However, naming the high school also serves a very important function. It indicates with whom the applicant studied and facilitates the use of the "old-boy network."

A common practice is to specify gender, age or physical attributes in job advertisements. Most firms will ask for a photograph of the applicant for their file.

All offices employ a man known as a Junior. This person is responsible for all miscellaneous errands. Juniors go to the bank, deliver documents (which makes courier services somewhat obsolete), purchase office supplies, etc. In many offices, the Junior also pays personal bills and makes bank deposits for individuals. However, this is not his job and is done only as a favor.

Each employee is responsible for paying for his or her personal long distance telephone calls, faxes, photocopies, etc. (Calls and faxes made regarding business are excluded.) At the end of the month, you might be expected to declare your personal calls and faxes. In some instances you are asked to keep track of personal photocopies on a nearby list. These amounts are then tallied and paid.

BENEFITS

Employees are given 15 days paid vacation following the first year of employment. This amount increases with time. In addition, there are 14 public holidays in Chile. If the holiday falls on a weekend, the worker is not compensated with a week day off. When an employee is absent from work due to illness, a *licencia* (doctor's note) must be presented upon returning to the office. Health care and social security entitlements are discussed in detail below. In general, benefits are not negotiated during the hiring process, only salary and bonuses.

Health Care

According to law, a portion of every employee's salary (seven percent) must be withheld for health care. The employee chooses the health care plan he or she wishes to join: the state system (FONASA) or one of the private plans called ISAPRES. Most salaried employees opt for an ISAPRE because the level of health care covered is substantially better than that provided by FONASA. There are a number of different ISAPRE plans from which the employee can choose. The plan is not tied to the place of employment.

AFPs

The Chilean social security system is one of the most modern and envied systems in Latin America. Contributions to the system by foreign personnel under a work contract generally must be paid by both the company and the foreigner. However, if the foreign worker has social security outside Chile with basic provisions for illness, pension, disability and death, then he or she may be exempt from making contributions. The AFP (pension) system is structured so that Chileans invest for old age during their working life ("pay as you go") and their savings are kept in individual accounts handled by private pension funds that compete against each other. So, if you do join the Chilean system, it is important to do your homework and study the current and past performances of these funds. Under the law, an employee must contribute 10 percent of his or her net taxable income, up to a certain maximum. However, additional payments may be made to your AFP tax-free, up to a certain limit. Those wishing to surpass this limit or make a separate investment, may make additional contributions to the AFP or open a separate savings account (linked to the performance of the fund) with the same institution.

LEGALITIES

It is illegal to work in Chile while on a tourist visa. If you are already in Chile on a tourist visa, you can apply at the Ministry of the Interior—Extranjeria (Foreigners Section) for: a) a Temporary Residence visa, but only if you have relatives in Chile or plan to make a sizable investment in Chile, b) a Resident Under Contract visa or c) a Student visa. However, the proper procedure is to apply for the correct visa at a Chilean consulate prior to your trip. The paperwork is substantial. You need a valid passport, a health certificate, a certificate from the police stating your good conduct and a notarized work contract or a letter of registration from the educational institution that you will be attending.

FREELANCE WORK

It may appeal to you to do freelance work while in Chile, especially if your spouse has a work permit. Every time you receive payment for your work, you must give your client a receipt of honorarium or Boleta de Honorarios. You save the copy for your income tax declaration. You cannot be paid for work unless you provide your client with a *boleta*. Earnings are generally subject to a 10 percent withholding tax, but you can negotiate with your clients whether your fee is *líquido* (net: the amount after the withholding tax) or *bruto* (gross: the full amount from which you yourself will pay the 10% withholding). The income recorded on your *boletas* must be reported on your annual income tax declaration.

The paperwork is really overwhelming to get a Boleta de Honorarios, but well worth the effort. First, you must apply for an RUT (taxpayer identification number), which in and of itself requires major paperwork. Having been assigned an RUT you can order the actual book of receipts, the *talonario de boletas*, at any small printer's shop. You must include your address, full name, field of activity and RUT. Every *boleta* in this book must be stamped by the Servicio de Impuestos Internos, the Chilean internal tax collector. In order to get that stamp, an application called Iniciación de Actividades must be completed. Do not be scared off though, the paperwork required in Chile is no more excessive than that required to work in other countries. Give yourself plenty of time to get the necessary papers and have it all approved.

The Boleta de Honorarios must not be confused with the sales receipt or *boleta*, which every merchant or service provider will give you for almost all transactions (as mandated by law). Unless you need them to justify expenses or to exchange an item, these *boletas* are of no use, but they multiply like rabbits after a few purchases.

When buying at large supermarkets, gas stations or stores selling intermediary goods you may be asked "*boleta o factura?*" meaning "sales receipt or invoice?" The *factura* or invoice is for individuals or corporations that can get VAT credit from the tax authorities. If you do not qualify, just answer "*boleta*" and pocket your newly acquired piece of paper.

CURRENCY

As in many other countries, periods distinguish thousands and commas denote fractions when writing numbers (for example, $5.000,30 is five thousand pesos and thirty cents). For simplicity, cents have

Many large ticket items are still priced in terms of UFs, a holdover from the time when Chile suffered from high inflation.

been eliminated in accounting records. In Chilean slang, 1 *luca* is equivalent to 1,000 pesos and 1 *guatón* (fat one) is equal to 1 million pesos. A Gabriela is a 5,000 peso bill (graced by the portrait of poet Gabriela Mistral). The Unidad de Fomento, or UF, as it is commonly called, is a value unit that was created to account for inflation at a time when it had reached double-digit levels. The UF almost became a parallel currency. Most large ticket items that are paid over a long period of time, such as real estate, cars, rent, etc., are still priced in UFs or in the "peso equivalent of the UF." One UF is equal to a determined amount of pesos and this figure changes daily. Newspapers list the value of the UF in each issue. Also be careful to note that dates are written day/month/year.

TAXES

If a foreigner resides in Chile for six consecutive months in a calendar year or for more than a total of six months in two consecutive years, he or she is considered a resident and must pay taxes. Taxes for residents must be paid on income from either Chilean or foreign sources. Foreigners working in Chile, however, are only subject to taxes on their Chilean income during the first three years of residence, and this period may be extended. Beyond this extra period foreigners are subject to tax on their worldwide income. Taxes are annual, and are calculated on December 31 of each year. Tax returns must be filed in April each year on income earned in the preceding calendar year.

A real estate tax is levied on all property bought in Chile. The amount due is equal to two percent of the fiscal valuation, and is payable in four installments (April, June, September, November).

Value Added Tax or IVA is 18 percent in Chile and is already included in published prices (with the exception of capital goods and intermediary goods, where price is expressed as $ + IVA). By paying with US dollars, traveler's checks or a non-Chilean credit card, a foreigner can avoid the hefty IVA charge at most hotels in Chile. Keep this in mind at check-out time.

— Chapter Ten —

SETTLING IN

PLEASE PUT HIM
DOWN IN FRONT
OF THE T.V.

WELCOME TO SANTIAGO

If you've made the decision to move to Chile, you are in for a wonderful experience. However, some adjustments will be necessary with respect to day-to-day living. Because most expatriates will be living in Santiago, this chapter will begin with a focus on the capital. Specific details concerning life in other major cities are addressed in Chapter 12.

Santiago, the capital, is also the largest city in Chile. Roughly one-third of the country's population of 14 million lives in Santiago. It is a sprawling city in the Central Valley which has spread out to the base of the Andes Mountains in the east. The western part of the city lies about 150 kilometers (90 miles) from the Pacific coast.

The Santiago metropolitan region is made up of over 30 *comunas,* or municipalities, each with its own mayor. When Chileans talk about Santiago most often they are referring to the greater Santiago area. However, in political terms, Santiago Centro is a specific municipality that administers the downtown area.

The more affluent Santiaguinos began moving closer and closer to the base of the *cordillera* (mountain range) in increasing numbers in the early 1980s. It was during this time that new neighborhoods hidden deep in the hills were being rapidly developed. This area is referred to as uptown and includes the neighborhoods of La Dehesa, Lo Barnechea and Santa María de Manquehue. It is sometimes jokingly referred to as "the United States" because the houses, stores and layout resemble those of any neighborhood in California. Other affluent neighborhoods are Las Condes, Los Dominicos, El Golf, Vitacura and parts of Providencia. In such a class-based society, Chileans are able to form an immediate opinion about someone by their address. The subway, or Metro, runs only as far as Las Condes, so living in the nicer parts of Santiago requires a car.

Many foreigners also live in the nice middle-class areas of Providencia and Ñuñoa. There are some beautiful old houses and modern apartment buildings in these two municipalities. They are also better served by public transportation and located nearer to supermarkets and other stores.

Although people still live in downtown Santiago, it is primarily a business district. Some businesses have begun moving their offices to El Bosque, an area between Apoquindo Avenue and the river, just east of Tobalaba Avenue. These are very trendy office addresses and in the lunch hour nearby restaurants are swamped by Chilean yuppies.

CLIMATE

Due to the fact that Chile is in the southern hemisphere, the seasons are reversed from those in the northern hemisphere. Winter begins in April and September signals the advent of Spring. November 1 is a public holiday that marks the unofficial beginning of summer. Schools have summer vacation from Christmas until the end of February. Many offices close for vacation in February. If you arrive in Chile in January or February, it will be very difficult to locate people. Everyone returns to their regular schedule in March as the temperatures begin to drop.

In the central region, where Santiago is located, summer temperatures reach as high as 34°C (93°F). However, it is a very dry heat and is not extremely uncomfortable. Spring and fall are moderate and quite pleasant. Winter, however, is cold and damp as this is also the rainy season. Temperatures hover just above freezing, leaving you with a chill that cannot be shaken.

Chileans often complain about the cold and you will often hear the term *friolento* (a person who becomes cold quite easily). Make sure that you have plenty of blankets and long underwear to prepare for winter. Residents of northern Wisconsin, Chicago and even Moscow have complained that the coldest winter they've ever experienced was in Santiago.

In northern Chile the weather remains mild all year long. In the Lake District, it rains most of the year and never gets really hot in the summer, although there are pronounced seasons. The extreme southern portion of the country experiences very cold winters accompanied by snow and high winds, and during the summer months the temperature averages 15°C (59°F).

Chilean time is four hours behind Greenwich Mean Time during mid-March to September (daylight savings time during the winter) and is three hours behind for the remainder of the year. Because of Chile's elongated shape, the entire country is in the same time zone.

POLLUTION

The major health concern in Santiago is air pollution. Although vehicle exhaust and emissions from nearby factories contribute to the smog, dust is another serious culprit. Santiago is a very dry and dusty city and studies have recommended paving more roads to address the pollution problem. Others argue this would raise temperatures. A thick layer of smog becomes trapped by the mountain range. In the morning the smog is heaviest in the downtown area, yet by late afternoon hangs heavy over the affluent neighborhoods at the base of the mountains. For this reason it is said to be "democratic" pollution. The situation is worse in winter when children and older citizens are severely affected. Rain is the only effective manner of ridding the city of the smog. Following a downpour, the sky is clear and the snow-capped mountains can be seen from the city. For those who enjoy working out, it is healthier to do so indoors. When Susan's office moved she opted to walk to work, only 10 minutes away. Within three days she came down with a terrible cold from the pollution and decided that it was in her best interest to take the Metro two stops. Those who can, leave the city on weekends. Once out of Santiago the air is clean and fresh, especially along the coast.

Anti-Pollution Measures and Restricción

You may be surprised to learn that the situation is much better than it was during the 1980s! During that era, particles in the air reached 340 micrograms per cubic meter. In 1996, there were only 12 days when particle levels surpassed the 300 level. Since 1990, 13 pollution fighting measures have been announced, nevertheless, the smog remains a very serious problem. When levels surpass 300, the government declares a pre-emergency and institutes safety measures, which include widening *restricción* and closing down factories in and around the city. Yet critics, primarily doctors, point out that the smog is already quite harmful when the levels reach 100 and therefore pre-emergency levels should be lowered.

Restricción is a government imposed system which restricts the use of vehicles in an attempt to reduce pollution levels. It covers all vehicles without catalytic converters and is in effect Monday

The government has instituted car pool lanes called Vias Vierdes along the Costanera in Santiago to help reduce congestion and pollution.

through Friday with the exception of public holidays. Each day of the week is assigned two numbers for the period of one month, for example: Monday 2 and 6; Tuesday 4 and 9, etc. Any vehicle whose license plate ends with either of the two numbers is not allowed to drive within the Santiago metropolitan region from 6:30 a.m. until 7:00 p.m. Every month the numbers are changed so that no vehicle is forced to have *restricción* every Friday. In pre-emergency situations, the government extends *restricción* by adding two more numbers for each day.

However, as the pollution problem has become more serious the government has recently made a number of proposals to toughen the policy. When you arrive in Santiago, make sure to get current information regarding this policy. The numbers are well advertised in newspapers and on television and the policy is enforced. Drivers caught breaking the law must pay a hefty fine.

Litter

You may be shocked by the amount of litter thoughtlessly strewn about, especially in common public areas and along highways. Driving along the road you will undoubtedly see people toss garbage from car or bus windows. Although Chileans keep their homes and private areas neat and tidy, sadly there is a lack of understanding that common areas are their responsibility too. This can be blamed partly on successive governments that have failed to institute anti-littering campaigns. Chileans are under the impression that it is solely the government's responsibility to clean up and maintain public areas. Municipalities hire laborers to sweep up the plazas, sidewalks and streets, but clearly this is not enough.

EARTHQUAKES

Tremors in Chile are quite common and if you do not come from an area prone to earthquakes it will be a frightening adjustment. Chileans swear that a major earthquake is destined to hit somewhere in the country every five years, but there is no scientific proof to support this claim. If you look closely, you will notice that Chileans take care in decorating their homes so that fragile items are secured and will not easily fall during a tremor. The last major earthquake to hit Santiago and the entire Central Valley was in 1985.

The best advice if one hits is to brace yourself in a door frame. Always leave shoes or slippers next to your bed while sleeping in case the floor is covered with broken glass. If you are in the city, do not run outside as there is a danger of being hit by falling electrical lines. All buildings in urban areas are built according to strict earthquake resistant codes. In rural areas where houses may be less resilient and power lines far away, it is best to be outside. It is always good to have bottled water on hand in case water mains are ruptured and contaminated. Chances are you will not experience a major earthquake during your stay, but you will notice the minor tremors and the numerous car alarms that they set off.

HOUSING

The first decision that you must make is whether to live in a house or an apartment. Many well-off Chileans prefer to live in apartment buildings because of the security they provide. Houses, in spite of the tall gates, are more susceptible to break-ins.

Apartment leases are normally signed on an annual basis, renewable with two months notice. A deposit equivalent to one or two months rent is customary. If a real estate agent is involved, you will have to pay him or her the equivalent of half of one month's rent for services. The landlord normally pays the real estate agent a similar amount.

Renters are responsible for paying *gastos comunes* (condo fees). These are paid directly to the building management on a monthly basis and are separate from rent, which is paid to the owner. This fee covers maintenance of the building, i.e., elevators, lights, etc. and pays the salaries of the building employees. In general, the more expensive your apartment, the higher the *gastos comunes*. It is computed in relation to the size of your apartment and may run anywhere from US$30 to US$200 and above depending on the services your building provides. When apartment-hunting, be sure to ask the amount of *gastos comunes*. When renting either a house or apartment, it is important to remember that kitchen appliances are generally not included. This means that you will have to purchase your own stove, refrigerator, microwave, etc.

Califont

Two other appliances that you will have to become very familiar with are the *califont* and the *estufa*. The *califont* is the gas water heater that is generally located in the kitchen or bathroom. This must be turned on and the pilot light lit every time you wish to use hot water (it should not be left on when not in use). When you turn on the hot water do not be surprised by the loud whooshing noise it makes as it ignites to heat the water. Getting the right water temperature can be somewhat tricky and if the appliance is old, temperature can change suddenly! One thing to remember is that the lower the stream of water, the hotter it will be as there is less water to heat, so sometimes it helps to turn the hot water higher in order to cool it off. Each *califont* has a personality of its own and you will only achieve the perfect shower through trial and error. If you have the option, a newer model is preferred because older *califonts* are prone to gas leaks and ventilation problems.

Estufas

The *estufa* is a space heater that is a must for every room in the house. Some new houses may have central heating, but in general it tends to be very expensive. Because most Chileans have only two or three *estufas*, some rooms are not used during the winter, especially large rooms that are difficult to heat.

There are three types of *estufas*: gas, electric and kerosene (*parafina*). Kerosene is the older and cheaper type, and tends to be the most popular. Once the wick is lit, it glows red for hours. Kerosene can be purchased at most gas stations (buy your own reusable container). Because the kerosene gives off an unpleasant smell, many people put a bowl of water with eucalyptus leaves or orange rinds on top of the heater. It should never be used in a small room and doors to other rooms should be left open a crack for air circulation. When extinguishing the flame, major fumes are emitted by the *estufa*. Therefore, they should only be extinguished in a large, outdoor area.

Electric *estufas* are an expensive way to heat a room because they are not very efficient. However, they are the easiest, cleanest and most convenient to use. It is tempting to purchase an electric *estufa* because all you need to do is plug it in, but be prepared for a very large electric bill.

Gas *estufas* are cheaper than electric *estufas* and more convenient than kerosene *estufas*. Some use gas that is piped into your home directly, but most use refillable gas canisters. Arrangements can be made with any of a number of companies that will pick up the old gas canisters and deliver new ones when needed. Or, you can purchase a new canister from a truck that passes up and down the streets. The workers bang the canisters to alert you of their arrival. The gas *estufa*, like the kerosene *estufa*, also works by using an open flame, but it gives off no fumes and can be extinguished inside.

Recently, catalytic *estufas* have been introduced. They use cleaner gas as fuel and are healthier and safer, but more expensive.

Although most *estufas* are relatively safe, special care should be taken if you have small children. Most of the fires caused by *estufas* are the result of carelessness. They should not be used in bathrooms, left unattended or placed near anything flammable, and they should be turned off before going to bed. Some mornings may be unbearable, as bathrooms tend to trap the cold, but that is part of the charm of living in Chile.

Utilities

Utilities are very efficient and function regularly with only minor disturbances, if any. Water is potable. Susan drank water directly from the tap and never had any health problems. Most people arriving in a new country will have minor stomach upsets as they become accustomed to the change in overall diet and water. If you are in Chile for a long period of time, you may want to risk a bout of *chilenitis*. There are no long lasting implications and after an episode you should become immune to some of the common bacteria. However, if diarrhea persists you should see a doctor.

MEDICAL SERVICES

The quality of health care depends upon whether the facilities are private or public. Private hospitals and clinics provide excellent care, modern facilities and high-tech equipment. You should have no trouble finding a doctor who speaks English, French, German, Italian, etc. Call your embassy for all the relevant information. The most highly respected hospitals are Clínica Las Condes, Clínica Alemana and Clínica Vitacura. The same highly qualified doctors also work at public hospitals and clinics, but the level of care is much lower because of the substandard facilities and equipment available.

In case of a medical emergency, most Chileans call the police first (dial 133) because they respond immediately. There is a direct number to request an ambulance listed on the front page of the phone book, but the police can also have one sent to you. Over the past few years private emergency services have emerged. Members pay a monthly fee and are registered with the service. Non-members may also call and request help, although the fee will be higher. These services began with heart patients, but have spread to include other medical conditions and accidents. Some services also have contracts with individual schools and corporations.

Pharmacies in Chile sell medicine and a few sundry items. Toiletries can be purchased at other stores. Most medicines can be bought over the counter without a prescription. In fact, if you're not feeling well you can discuss the symptoms with the pharmacist, who will suggest medicines.

DOCUMENTATION

Depending on your citizenship, either a visa issued by a Chilean embassy, or a tourist permit good for 90 days (note: not three months) and issued upon arrival will be required. If you are planning a longer stay in Chile, a specific visa will be required. For information call the nearest Chilean embassy or consulate. Chile has embassies throughout the Americas, in most European countries and in several Asian countries. If you are traveling as a tourist, a return ticket, or ticket to a third country is required before you will be allowed to enter.

Each Chilean has an identification card called a Carnet de Identidad and a RUN (Rol Unico Nacional), which is a number assigned to each person at birth. This number is used for all official documents, i.e., *carnet*, passport, taxpayer ID number, driver's license and voter ID card. Chileans commonly refer to this number as their *carnet* number, not their RUN. A RUT is a taxpayer ID number which is granted to individuals and corporations, both local and foreign, who are conducting business in Chile and must pay taxes.

After you have received your visa, you will be issued a Carnet de Identidad with a foreigner ID number and you will be requested to register with a special section of the police that deals with immigration, called Policía Internacional.

CURRENCY AND MONEY
The Chilean currency is the peso which fluctuates between 450 and 460 to the US dollar. Coins come in denominations of 1 peso (worth very little and very rarely used), 5 pesos, 10 pesos, 50 pesos and 100 pesos (roughly $0.25). Bills are issued in 500, 1,000, 2,000, 5,000 and 10,000 peso (roughly $25.00) denominations. If you are buying a cheap item, small bills and coins are appreciated, especially in the markets.

US dollars are not widely accepted, so you will have to change money upon arrival. It is customary for traveler's checks to trade at a slightly lower rate than cash. You will need to go to a *casa de cambio* as banks may or may not perform this service. If provided, the bank will always offer a lower exchange rate than the *casa de cambio*. For a fee, the *casa de cambio* will also issue or cash a check in US dollars. There are a number of *casas de cambio* along Agustinas Street between Morandé Street and Estado Street in the center and on Pedro de Valdivia Avenue, just north of Providencia Avenue in the Providencia district. You will undoubtedly be approached by hawkers whispering "Dolares" as you walk down Agustinas. They do not offer better rates than the *casas de cambio* and are not as trustworthy. One American who worked on Wall Street was cheated by one of these guys who had rigged his calculator. Due to the number of zeros involved, one can get confused quite easily. Also, do remember to be careful upon leaving a *casa de cambio*. Experienced pickpockets prey on Chileans and foreigners alike exiting banks and *casas de cambio*.

If you have a RUT, you can open a checking and/or savings account at any Chilean bank. *Casas de cambio* close for two hours for lunch around 2:00 p.m. Banks close for the day at 2:00 p.m. on weekdays and do not open at all on Saturdays. ATMs are abundant.

Bills

Most people pay their utility bills in person. Each bill lists payment centers on the reverse side. Payment can usually be made at a specific bank, supermarket or utility office. Payment can be made either by check or in cash. You can also instruct your bank to deduct utility charges directly from your current account. Payment by mail is rare.

Checks

Many Chileans make all purchases with a check. Laws against writing bad checks are very strict and it is considered a serious offense. Most offenders will very likely wind up in jail and their credit will be ruined. Therefore, checks are accepted everywhere, i.e., stores, restaurants, gas stations, etc., provided that you show your *carnet* or passport. People normally write their *carnet* and telephone number on the back of the checks they issue, to facilitate the transaction.

CRIME

Crime in Santiago is similar to that in any other major city. Pickpockets are a problem, particularly in the downtown area and especially if you look like an easy target, i.e., a lost tourist. You should not stroll through downtown after business hours, especially near the Plaza de Armas, which can become quite seedy at night. A few years back, the municipality of Santiago installed overhead police cameras in the downtown area in order to deter crime. Their presence, along with other measures, has helped reduce crime in this zone by 20 percent.

Another area that should be avoided at night is the Santa Lucia Hill. With all its nooks and crannies, it is an ideal location for muggings. Even during the day, women should not visit this park alone. This park is perfectly safe if you go as part of a group and the view from the top of the hill is well worth the steep climb.

As in other countries, the poorer neighborhoods (with higher rates of unemployment and drug abuse) tend to have higher crime rates. Being alert and knowing where you are are the best forms of prevention. Santiaguinos arc quick to point out, however, that their city has a murder rate of 3.3 per 100,000 inhabitants, much lower than other Latin American and North American cities, which have rates over seven per 100,000. Furthermore, the rate of robberies per 100,000 residents is 880, much lower than Miami or New York, which have rates over 1,500.

The Police

In any type of emergency the best advice is to call the police first at 133. They will respond quickly and direct your call to any other agency needed, such as the fire department or an ambulance service. Bribes are not common practice in Chile and under no circumstances should you attempt to bribe a Carabinero. This will only get you into trouble. Chileans refer to the police as *pacos*, and although not an insult, the slang term is not preferred by the police themselves. The other branch of the Chilean police force is called Policía de Investigaciones (Investigations Unit). These are the plain-clothed police, or detectives.

Fire Department

You may often see Bomberos, as firemen are called, out collecting donations in the streets. This is because all firemen in Chile are volunteers, with the exception of paid professional fire departments at the airport, in the armed forces and in certain industries. Bomberos are highly respected in Chile and some units are more prestigious than others. Several units are comprised of members from certain groups (the French Company) or from certain professions (i.e., lawyers). All volunteers undergo rigorous training and there is a strict hierarchical

161

Firemen in Chile are volunteers and some companies are organized according to nationality or profession.

order within each company. Although they are not paid a salary, fire fighters receive other forms of compensation, for example, meals or shelter. Fire departments are funded by the State, by members' contributions, by public donations and by revenue from lotteries that by law must contribute a certain portion to charities, etc. However, most units run on very tight budgets, so feel free to donate!

EDUCATION

Overall, Chile has a good education system. Not surprisingly, private schools have the best test scores. An education reform has recently been initiated in order to improve the quality of education, particularly in the public schools. There are three types of schools – public or *pública* (government-funded and administered by the municipalities); private or *particular* (privately funded and run); and subsidized private or *particular subvencionada* (government-funded but privately administered). *Escuelas* (primary schools) provide education for the first eight grades and *colegios* or *liceos* (high schools) the next four. Students in the same homeroom become very close as they study as one group for the entire eight or even 12 years.

In general, private schools provide the best education. However, this is not a hard and fast rule as there are a number of high quality public schools. Some upper-class private schools are extremely conservative and will not accept illegitimate children or children of parents who have separated. Public schools and subsidized private schools cannot exclude anyone because they receive government funding. If a foreign child is a legal resident of Chile (i.e., has a valid visa) he or she should not be legally barred from attending either a private or public school.

There are also a number of foreign schools and several foreign-language schools. There are German, Italian, French, and English schools where the majority of students are Chilean, yet practically all instruction is in the foreign language. Your embassy should be able to provide you with the relevant information.

Universities

The Chilean university system has a very good reputation, built primarily on the prominence of the two main traditional universities, Universidad Católica and Universidad de Chile. Degree programs in medicine, law, engineering, economics, business (*ingeniero comercial*), agriculture and mining and marine sciences are among the best in the region. For this reason, many Latin Americans choose to study in Chile.

Prior to the 1980s, Chile had only a small number of traditional universities that received full or partial state funding. The military government decided to introduce competition into the system. Anyone who complied with certain requirements could open and run a university. These "new" universities are separate from the traditional universities, but are under their supervision until firmly established. Today there are over 30 traditional and new universities in Chile. The traditional universities enjoy name recognition, are more prestigious and are assumed to have better professors. (It is common in Chile for practicing professionals to teach at the universities.) Some of the new universities are gaining prestige, but this is a slow process. In general, it is easier to be admitted into a new university, so there is an element of elitism for students and alumni of traditional universities.

For years, students from neighboring countries have come to Chile to receive a higher education. With the increase in the number of universities, there are now even greater opportunities for foreigners to study in Chile. Some universities provide tailored programs for foreign students, so it is a good idea to shop around for the best program.

University students in Chile enter a degree program that takes roughly four to seven years to complete. Almost all classes pertain to the student's chosen field, unlike in some other countries where a wide range of topics is studied. Therefore, everyone studying the same subject knows each other but do not have much interaction with students in other fields. In fact, different "schools" (the school of economics, the school of journalism, etc.) are located on various campuses, thereby segregating the students further. A *práctica* (internship) and a thesis are required of all students, most often during the final year of study.

Upon graduation, a *título* (degree) or a *licencia* (license) is conferred that allows the graduate to practice a specific profession. A person without this specific degree or license would be prohibited from working in the field. In this sense, it is very different from the system in the United States where students receive academic degrees that are quite flexible and allow the student to practice a wide range of professions. This difference explains the confusion surrounding questions about careers. In the United States, the question is "What do you do?" and the answer usually relates to one's current position, for example, "I'm a Marketing Director for (name of company)." In Chile, the question is "What are you?" and refers to your profession in general, not your specific job title. "I'm an economist, mathematician, an *ingeniero comercial*, etc."

There are two types of university entrance exams, the PAA (Prueba de Aptitud Académica) and the Prueba de Conocimientos Específicos. The PAA tests general knowledge of Spanish, mathematics and social sciences. The other exam covers specific subjects required for particular careers. Admission requirements for the traditional universities are tough; applicants must have high test scores and a good high school record. There are a limited number of spaces, so competition is fierce.

Spanish Programs

Spanish-language programs are also offered in Santiago, the best known being the North American-Chilean Institute. This institute offers both Spanish and English courses which allows for interaction between both groups. The Instituto Chileno-Británico and the Goethe Institut also have good Spanish programs, in addition to teaching English and German respectively.

Volunteering

For those who wish to do volunteer work in Chile, there is a wide selection of opportunities. The best place to start is with the Guía de la Solidaridad. This guide lists all the charity and volunteer organizations in Chile. It is provided along with the telephone book and is the best source for those who wish to do something positive with their extra time.

DRESS

Older women continue to wear skirts, although younger Chilean women are now heavily influenced by fashion trends in the United States and Europe. Previously, shorts were worn only at the beach, but you will now see them all over Santiago during the summer. It is advisable not to bring white clothing, as it gets dirty very quickly due to the pollution and dust. For this same reason, shoes tend to suffer from more wear and tear than elsewhere.

Winters mean low temperatures both inside and outside. You must bundle up during the winter and heavy sweaters are a good idea. Men often wear sweater vests under their suitcoats and this would be a worthwhile investment. However, the temperature outside is never radically different from that inside, therefore heavy winter coats are not necessary. Remember, the temperature rarely dips below freezing.

School Clothes

All schoolchildren are required to wear uniforms, whether in public or private schools. University students are expected to dress nicely for class. Most wear trendy casual clothes and jeans are acceptable, but ratty T-shirts and shorts are not appropriate. Hats are never worn indoors and shoes are never removed during class. The professor has the right to ask you to leave if he finds your dress unacceptable.

SHOPPING

Large, modern shopping malls are popping up in Santiago, although many individual stores still line both major and small streets. In Santiago there are two major shopping malls in Las Condes. In Chile, prices for high-quality items, especially clothes and imported toiletries can be quite high. In fact, many women exchange expensive shampoo and conditioner sets as gifts. There are, of course, a wide range of low-priced items of lower quality. In addition to the shopping malls, stores along Providencia Avenue and along other major streets in Las Condes offer high-quality items. The major department stores are Falabella, Almacenes París and Ripley.

When making a purchase three different salespeople wait on you. The person who makes the sale brings your purchase to the *caja* where you pay and get a stamped receipt. That salesperson then transfers your purchase to *empaque*. You present your receipt at *empaque* in order to pick up the wrapped goods.

The downtown area is full of *galerias*, large indoor networks of passageways lined with many small shops. Other areas that sell less expensive goods are Patronato Street and the outlet mall in Maipú. *Mercados persas* or just *persas* are permanent flea markets/bazaars. Each *persa* is made up of a number of small stalls selling almost anything at very low prices. You may want to check out the Persa Estación by the Estación Central. Also, running along the entire length of Avenida Providencia and the Alameda are very cheap used clothing stores. Most of the used clothing is imported from Europe. If you enjoy rummage stores, they are worth a peek for bargains. Except for the malls, all stores close Saturday at 2:00 p.m. and are closed all day Sunday.

Clothing

Because well-made ready-to-wear clothing can be quite expensive and labor costs are still quite low, having clothes made by a tailor is a good option. In fact, this may be the best choice for a man's suit.

Also, because it is difficult to return items once purchased, make sure you buy the right size and that you like it.

Women's clothes tend to be smaller than in the United States and large women may have a problem finding clothes that fit. They also tend to fit differently in the hips and waist. Ask about a good *modista* (seamstress) for tailor-made outfits for ladies. Women's shoes also run small, usually up to a US size 8 or European size 38.

Crafts

Ferias are markets or fairs where you can find Chilean crafts. Some popular ones are Feria Santa Lucía across from Santa Lucía Hill, Pueblo de Artesanos de Los Dominicos at the end of Avenida Las Condes, and La Aldea de Vitacura on Vitacura Avenue.

MAIDS

Many middle-class and upper-class families have maids or nannies. Most Chileans use the terms interchangeably, but technically nannies take care of the children in addition to doing the housework. In the past, most maids lived with the family, but today the number is split between live-in (*puertas adentro*) maids and those who come only for the day (*puertas afuera*). Most maids are expected to clean, cook, do laundry, iron and take care of the children. They wear their own clothes, but if you would like them to wear a uniform, you are expected to provide it. Most live-in maids do not work on Sundays. The current salary for a full-time live-in maid is about US$200 per month.

Most of these women come from low-income backgrounds and a large percentage come from the Temuco area and are of Indian origin. Peruvian maids working illegally in Chile are becoming a common addition to Chilean households. Maids who work on a daily basis often have their own families and live in lower-income neighborhoods. A maid who has been with the same family for a very long time is practically considered a member of that family and is treated well.

Families who are searching for a maid use the "nana network." Most maids have a friend or a relative who is looking for work with a family. If you are looking to hire a maid you can either ask around or go to an agency. The agencies may provide more guarantees, but regardless of how the maid is hired, you would be well advised to insist on talking to her former employers. Although most are trustworthy, there are always a few bad apples. You may want to keep a copy of her Carnet de Identidad. Finally, if you go on vacation ask her to return the keys. You may find your maid to be loyal and trustworthy, but you can never be sure who has access to her keys.

Legal Aspects

Laws protecting maids state, among other things, that in addition to salary, an employer should contribute to the employees retirement fund and health care plan. Working hours, breaks and days off are also dictated by law. The government makes every attempt to ensure that these laws are observed and if a maid can prove non-compliance, her employer faces stiff financial penalties. Although a significant number of people circumvent the law, either by arrangement with the maid (i.e., she receives a higher salary but no contributions to health care) or because the maid is unaware of her rights, you should make sure you follow the local laws. For more details call the Ministry of Labor.

REPAIRMEN

Depending upon the rental agreement, you may be responsible for repairs in your home. Most likely, the landlord will handle major repairs, but you will have to take charge of minor problems. There are two options for finding a repairman (*maestro*). First, the telephone book has a long list of professional services under *reparaciones*. If the problem concerns electricity or gas, the best suggestion is to call the company or a professional service.

For other minor repairs, however, a cheaper alternative is to ask the *mayordomo* (superintendent) of the building or your maid if they

169

know anyone who can do the job. Most likely they can provide you with the name of a *maestro* who can fix "anything." It is important to ask someone you trust, because some *maestros* are much better than others, in terms of both ability and punctuality. Make sure you stress exactly what you want done, otherwise it may turn into a bigger project than desired. A common practice is for the *maestro* to come first to look at the problem and ask for money in advance to buy parts. He will set up a time to return to complete the project. Rarely will someone take the money and not do the job, especially if they were recommended by a friend. Also, using a false ID from a professional service to gain access to your house is not a common crime in Chile. Most *maestros* are trustworthy, but you should never leave them alone in your home.

A professional service can be paid by cash or check and you may tip the repairman. If you hire someone from a small shop or an independent *maestro* no tip is necessary.

MAIL

If you live in a house, or even in some apartment buildings, mail carriers often deliver mail to you directly. Technically, the carrier should be paid a small amount (a few pesos) for each piece of mail that is delivered. Most people pay a lump sum at the end of each month.

If you are having a large package sent from abroad, it will go through customs and once cleared, a notice will be sent to your address. The recipient must go to customs (near Parque O'Higgins) to pick it up in person, with a form of identification. If items can be sent separately in legal-size envelopes, they will not get stuck in customs and will be delivered right to your door.

CARTONEROS

If you live in a house, refuse should be placed outside your home the night before garbage collection. It is a good idea to place it up high (some people hang it from trees) to prevent stray dogs from shredding the bags and scattering litter all over the street. Also, you may hear, late at night, someone rummaging through your garbage. *Cartoneros* ride around the dark streets on their bicycle carts scavenging for anything that can be sold or recycled such as cardboard, glass, paper, etc. You may want to leave these items out separately so that they don't have to go through the garbage.

TRANSPORTATION

Metro
Santiago's Metro will eventually have five lines, which explains why the current lines are numbered 1, 2 and 5. Lines 3 and 4 are scheduled to be built later. Line 1 runs directly across the city from east to west, passing through the center, along Providencia to Las Condes. Lines 2 and 5 run perpendicular to Line 1 and serve heavily populated middle-class and lower middle-class neighborhoods. Service is efficient, but during rush hour (8:00–9:30 a.m. and 6:00–7:30 p.m.) demand exceeds space and the cars are very crowded. It is best to force your way to the door before you arrive at your station, as it is not the custom for those blocking the doors to step off and let you exit.

Buses
Buses in Chile are called *micros* and in Santiago they have all been painted yellow although they are owned and operated by numerous individuals and companies. The cost of a ride is posted in the front window of each bus but exact change is not necessary. The bus driver will pass you a small ticket called a *boleto* which has a number and should be kept in case the bus is checked. Bus drivers earn a percentage of the money collected from the daily revenues of their specific bus. Some bus drivers have been known to collect *boletos* from disembarking passengers. By reissuing a previously used ticket, the driver can keep the full fare. When a bus is checked, the numbers

should be relatively close to each other. On a particularly crowded bus some passengers may board through the rear doors. Unable to pay the driver themselves, the money will be passed from hand to hand until it makes its way to the driver. The *boleto* and any change will be returned in the same manner.

Figuring out which bus you need to take can be somewhat tricky at first and the ride itself can be an experience. Signs are posted in the front window of every bus listing all the streets on its route. Therefore, the trick is to know major streets before and after your desired stop. The other option is to stop the bus and ask the driver if he goes where you are going, which is a very common practice. (¿Pasa por ...?) Once you become familiar with the geography of Santiago it will be much easier and you'll be hopping on and off buses like any Santiaguino. Buses will generally pick you up on any corner, except on Providencia Avenue and Alameda Avenue where buses have been assigned specific stops. A few other main thoroughfares like Vicuña McKenna also have designated stops as you get farther away from the city center.

The bus ride itself may prove interesting. Hawkers often board the bus selling ice cream, candy, pencils, etc. (They request permission from the bus driver first and do not pay.) Others may board with guitars or other musical instruments and play and/or sing. Prior to the performance many may tell you a sob story about how they are former prisoners trying to stay on the right side of the law. Most likely a few are telling the truth, but some use it as a ploy. Following the performance they will walk the length of the bus looking for tips. If you liked the performance, pay accordingly. Occasionally a deaf person may board and distribute plastic cards with calendars or sayings to each passenger. Once they are all passed out, he goes back to collect the money. You are expected to return the card if you don't want to make a donation. A number of people have remarked on how much they enjoyed riding buses because the rides were never boring.

Taxis

Taxis in Santiago are black with yellow roofs and run on meters. In general, you should never negotiate a fixed price beforehand. There is an abundance of cabs and for the most part they are very safe. Taxis are no longer allowed to enter a certain eight block area in the center without a passenger. Thus, if you are looking for a taxi and are within this radius you must look for a taxi letting a passenger off. Of course, as a result of Chilean ingenuity, some cab drivers actually pay people to ride in the back of the taxi so that they can enter the zone in order to pick up higher fare passengers.

If it is late at night or you need a taxi to pick you up at someone's home you should call a radiotaxi. You must pay a surcharge, but it is safe and prompt. Tourist taxis are commonly found at major hotels. The ride may be more luxurious, but the fare will be higher. Meters are not used in tourist taxis, so negotiate the price beforehand.

The Airport

When arriving at the Santiago airport (officially named "Comodoro Arturo Merino Benítez," but commonly referred to as Pudahuel after the neighborhood where it is located), there are a number of options to get to the city which is about a 30 minute drive. Airport taxis are available and charge a fixed rate. A coupon must be purchased from the taxi counter beforehand. A cheaper alternative is a Transfer. This is a minivan that takes about four people to different destinations within the same part of Santiago. This service is provided by both the Chilean airlines and private companies. The ticket is also purchased at the company's counter located on the arrival level. You must tell them what part of Santiago you are going to and they will tell you which van to board. If you are the first to be dropped off, it's as quick as a taxi, if you are the last, it's about 15 minutes longer. The cheapest way to get into the city is to take an airport bus that will drop you off at either the Los Heroes Metro stop, or at a bus terminal downtown.

If you need a ride to the airport all three forms of transportation are readily available in the opposite direction. Airport taxis are available at most large hotels. Any regular taxi will also take you to the airport, but some will most likely want to negotiate a fixed price beforehand. If you have a clear understanding of the value of Chilean currency you can negotiate a good price. The taxi drivers will try to make money, but will not try to rob you blind.

Colectivos

Colectivos look exactly like the black and yellow cabs but have a sign and number plate on top of the roof. These cars run predetermined routes and pick up as many passengers as will fit into the car. The cost is maybe double that of a bus, but far cheaper than a private taxi.

Driving

Driving in Santiago and along the Pan American Highway can be a harrowing experience. The number of cars on Chilean roads has increased dramatically over the past 10 to 15 years as Chileans have become more affluent. This sudden increase in new drivers combined with badly marked lanes and some questionable road signs can make driving in Santiago difficult at first. Once you are familiar with the city and with driving patterns you should have no problem.

The biggest problem in Chile is that cars share the road with pedestrians, old trucks, carts, bicycles and stray dogs. Once Susan even drove past a person in a wheelchair on a hill at night, with neither lights nor a reflector! In spite of the fact that the government has built a number of overpasses for pedestrians, most choose to dash across major highways instead. Moreover, the Pan American Highway runs through many small towns where it serves as the main thoroughfare.

Getting a Driver's License

Many foreigners drive in Chile with a driver's license from their home country. Technically, an international driver's license should be obtained in the home country before leaving. Foreigners who expect to be in Chile for a long period of time should apply for a Chilean driver's license. This can be done at the office of the municipality in which you reside. You will need to present your Carnet de Identidad and take three tests: a written test in Spanish, a road test and a medical exam that checks vision, hearing and reflexes.

It is relatively easy to rent a car in any major city. Offices are located at airports, major hotels and downtown areas. A passport and valid driver's license from your own country or an international driver's license are required and most major credit cards are accepted.

Tickets

If you are pulled over by a Carabinero and given a ticket, your license will be taken away. You will be given the ticket and a summons to appear in court. You are allowed to drive on your ticket, unless the offense is very serious and your driving privileges have been revoked. In general, you must appear in the court of the municipality where the ticket was issued on the date specified and if found guilty a stiff penalty will be imposed. You cannot plead guilty at the time of the offense and pay the policeman. The municipality of Las Condes is

Bribery is not common practice in Chile and can bring with it strict penalties.

175

experimenting with new procedures to simplify the process, whereby if you plead guilty you may pay the fine at a bank. Because this is an experimental phase, check details with the municipality directly.

Cuidadores de Autos

Another common sight in Chile is the parking attendant, called a *cuidador de autos*. Anywhere you park your car, be it on the street or in a private lot, within seconds a man or woman with a little handkerchief and/or flashlight will run over to your car to help guide you in. They aren't really paying attention though, so don't rely on their assistance too much. Supposedly they watch the cars in their "sector" while the owners are gone to protect them from robberies. When leaving they once again help guide you out of your spot and it is customary to give them a small tip. Most gas stations in Chile are still full service, so a small tip should be given to the gas station attendant too.

10 de Julio

Auto repair shops are concentrated on one street, 10 de Julio. In fact, on any given day this street is filled with mechanics fixing cars randomly parked off to the side. If the first shop doesn't have the necessary part, the mechanic will direct you to one further down the street. At the first sign of car trouble, head for 10 de Julio; just about anything you need can be found here and it can be a fun experience.

PUBLIC TOILETS

Most public toilets do not supply toilet paper, so it is always a good idea to carry your own supply. Sewer systems in many older buildings and houses and in rural areas where septic tanks are used cannot adequately process toilet paper. Used toilet paper should be thrown into the wastebasket next to the toilet. If there is no wastebasket next to the toilet, it is a sign that toilet paper can be flushed.

— Chapter Eleven —

FREE TIME IN CHILE

A PROUD LITERARY HISTORY

There is no better way to get to know your host culture than through its arts and literature. However, in spite of the fact that Chile is a large producer of paper, books tend to be expensive because the publishing industry is small. Most books in Spanish are imported from Argentina, Mexico and Spain and subject to the hefty VAT tax. A number of used bookstores have popped up in major cities and there are a number of English bookstores (new and used) in the Providencia and Las Condes sections of Santiago.

Much of Chile's art and literature follows the European tradition. Chile is proudest of its poets, and with good reason. Some of the biggest names in Spanish poetry are from Chile. *La Araucana* is a famous epic poem written at the end of the 16th century by the Spanish soldier and poet Alonso de Ercilla y Zúñiga (1534–94), who was stationed in Chile. It describes the bravery of the Indians resisting the Spanish conquistadors.

Andrés Bello was born in Venezuela in the late 18th century, but lived most of his life in Chile. A celebrated poet, he also founded the Universidad de Chile and wrote the penal and civil codes which, to this day, are the basis of the codified law in Chile.

In the 19th century several exiles from other South American nations found refuge in Chile, the most distinguished being Rubén Darío. This Nicaraguan native settled in Chile in 1886, yet lived many years abroad and influenced numerous European poets.

One of the most famous Chilean poets is Gabriela Mistral (1889–1957), who in 1945 became the first Latin American to be awarded the Nobel Prize for Literature. Her real name was Lucila Godoy Alcayaga and she was a poor rural schoolteacher. She wrote about her village, Monte Grande, and the children of her school. Her poems are magnificent in their simple treatment of everyday topics.

Pablo Neruda (1904–73) won the Nobel Prize for Literature in 1971. He is best known and admired for his poetry about love, *Twenty Love Poems and a Song of Despair*, and his celebration of Latin American culture, *Heights of Machu Picchu*. Some writings are also political in nature, since he was a devoted communist. Topics include poverty and the plight of the factory worker. The Neruda Prize is given to a Chilean every November as a literary honor. The movie *Il Postino* is a semi-fictional account of Neruda in Italy and his attempts to create a poet out of an Italian postman.

Neruda was an avid collector and all three of his homes can be visited. The house overlooking the Pacific Ocean in the town of Isla Negra (south of Algarrobo) is now a museum with countless naval artifacts, including his highly prized collection of ships' mastheads.

The house high on a hill in Valparaíso is also worth a visit because of its distinct architectural design, wonderful collection of artifacts and beautiful view of the city and bay. The third is in the Bellavista neighborhood of Santiago and can be visited by appointment.

Jorge Edwards and José Donoso are members of the Latin American "Boom" (along with Mario Vargas Llosa and Gabriel García Márquez). The Boom was a period during the 1960s–1980s when a number of Latin American authors wrote internationally acclaimed books. Donoso and Edwards went into exile during the military dictatorship. Donoso (1925–96) was a novelist and short story writer. His book, *The House Next Door*, shows some of the suffering an exile faces. Jorge Edwards (1931–) was a lawyer and foreign service officer. He was Deputy Chief of Mission in France when Pablo Neruda was Ambassador. Later he was Chargé d'Affaires in Cuba. His most celebrated novel, *Persona Non-Grata*, tells about his experiences in Cuba and being kicked out by Castro.

Isabel Allende, who is a distant cousin of former President Salvador Allende, also went into exile. She is one of Latin America's most popular authors. Her most famous work, *The House of Spirits*, is the story of an eccentric, aristocratic Chilean family. It was a worldwide best seller and was made into a movie starring Meryl Streep, Jeremy Irons, Winona Ryder and Glenn Close.

Ariel Dorfman has achieved worldwide renown for his play *Death and the Maiden*. This story focuses on the confrontation between a torture victim and her tormentor. The play was made into a movie starring Sigourney Weaver and Ben Kingsley.

Following the return to democracy there has been a wave of new authors such as Alberto Fuguet, Jaime Collyer, Carlos Franz, and Ana María del Río, to name just a few.

Condorito

One of Chile's most famous exports to the rest of the Spanish-speaking world is the comic book *Condorito*. It relates the adventures of a character with the head of a condor, the bird of the Andes, yet lives in a human world, surrounded by other human-like characters.

CONTEMPORARY MUSIC

The Chilean music scene has swelled since the end of military rule. There is something for every taste, from traditional Chilean music to folk, blues, jazz and rock. There are countless folk groups. In the northern regions the music has been more heavily influenced by the native cultures. The instruments are interesting and include the *queña*, a flute made of a single reed, and the *zampoña*, a pipe made of reeds of different lengths bound with bright wool. The Mapuche in the south play the *kultrún*, a type of drum, the *trutruka*, a wind instrument made from a long piece of bamboo, and the *pifillka*, a whistle.

Inti Illimani is the most internationally celebrated Chilean band. Los Inti, as they are affectionately referred to in Chile, went into exile

Traditional Andean instruments like the zampoña *(pan flute) have been incorporated into current Chilean popular music.*

to Europe like many other artists during the military regime. Originally a protest folk group which used traditional instruments, over time Inti Illimani's music and arrangements have become much more sophisticated. They have incorporated elements of Latin American and European folk music with New Age and even classical music. No drive through the Andes is complete without Inti Illimani playing in the background. For those who don't understand much Spanish, listen to their instrumental CD "Imagination."

Quilapayún is the quintessential protest song folk group. It was very combative early on and some of its songs were anthems for the revolution, for instance "La Batea." Quilapayún also went into exile in Europe, where its members remain. With the passage of time their songs have also shifted away from their original hard-line stance.

Perhaps the most famous Chilean singer/songwriter was Violeta Parra. She was the mother of the New Song Movement, a cultural movement which swept the country in the late 1960s and early 1970s. It voiced the great hope for political and social change in Latin America. She incorporated traditional rhythms, instruments and musical forms with modern lyrics. Parra committed suicide in 1967, supposedly due to financial problems and the failure of a love affair. Her most famous song "Gracias a la Vida" (Thanks to Life) was also recorded and made popular in English by Joan Baez. Her brother Nicanor Parra is a famous poet and many other family members are well-known musicians.

Another member of the New Song Movement was the folk singer Víctor Jara. He was arrested during the coup and detained in the Estadio Chile. He bravely sang protest songs while being detained and was eventually killed. He is a martyr to many Chileans. His two most famous songs are the beautiful "Te recuerdo Amanda" and "Plegaria del Labrador."

On the other side of the political spectrum, Los Huasos Quincheros represented the conservative right and sang folk songs for the upper classes. They are the very definition of *cuico*.

181

Chilean rock was strong in the early 1980s, then lost steam for a few years, but is currently picking up again. The Chilean rock scene continues to be less creative than Argentinean rock, which is THE rock movement in Latin America. La Ley and Los Tres are two popular young Chilean rock groups.

Music Festivals

The Festival de la Canción de Viña del Mar, one of the most important popular music festivals in all of the Spanish-speaking world, takes place every year in the seaside resort town of Viña del Mar, not far from Santiago. It is primarily a contest for up-and-coming singers, yet is well-known for the big name international artists who headline the festival. It is broadcast on television throughout Latin America. Although the festival has been criticized for not including enough Chilean bands and for emphasizing mainstream Spanish pop music, it is nevertheless the main event of the summer in Viña, and for that matter in Chile. The Song Festival is held in the first or second week of February. It lasts for one week, with two performances daily, one in the afternoon and the other at night. More than 30,000 spectators fill the Quinta Vergara outdoor auditorium. The winner is presented with the Gaviota (seagull) Trophy.

The Semanas Musicales de Frutillar is another large musical event. It is a 10-day classical music festival held in the town of Frutillar near Puerto Montt in southern Chile. It begins the first week of February and highlights both Chilean and foreign classical musicians alike.

MEDIA

The media in Chile is mostly privately owned and is receiving increasing inflows of foreign capital. The Catholic Church has substantial weight in the Chilean media. The Catholic University's system of television channels throughout Chile rivals that of the state-run channels and its revenues are larger. The Catholic University channel and another channel half-owned and wholly managed by a devout businessman have refused to run ads from the Health Ministry warning Chileans to take precautions against AIDS (SIDA in Spanish). The church's approach is to promote abstinence and fidelity to one's spouse. The church also has interest in a number of radio stations. Most newspapers in Chile rarely print articles on abortion or birth control.

Print Media

El Mercurio, the leading opinion-making newspaper, is very conservative. It is indirectly influenced by the church. It is considered a serious and traditional paper like *The New York Times* or *The London*

Kiosks offer a wide selection of local and foreign newspapers and magazines.

Times. Another leading Santiago newspaper *La Tercera* is owned by a group of Arab businessmen. This paper has been conservative in its treatment of topics like divorce and sex education. Nevertheless, *La Tercera* and another daily, *Las Ultimas Noticias,* are colorful and appeal to the masses. *La Nación* is a semi-official paper that has a small readership. *La Segunda* and *La Hora* come out in the afternoon and carry late-breaking news. It is common to hear the call of hawkers selling *La Segunda* in the downtown area in the afternoon. There are two very important financial papers, *El Diario Financiero* and *Estrategia*. Outside Santiago, every good-sized town has its own newspaper.

News Magazines

There are several news magazines published in Chile. *Hoy* is associated with the Christian Democratic Party. *Ercilla* and *Qué Pasa* tend to sympathize with the right. *Cosas* and *Caras* both provide a peculiar mix of gossip and in-depth interviews with important people; for example you might find a story about European royalty next to a great interview with President Frei.

In general, Chileans have access to a free press. However, at times, it has been subject to censorship. A recent case involving *La Tercera* reflects the public's opposition to any kind of censorship. A drug-related case was being tried in Chile and some members of the judiciary had been implicated. The courts slapped a gag order on the Chilean press, preventing it from covering the trial. *La Tercera* set up a website in the United States in order to legally cover the trial. Unable to control the flow of information, the government relented and revoked the gag order.

Foreign Language Media

For the die-hard expatriate there is an English language newspaper called *News Review* published twice a week, on Wednesday and Saturday. It contains events for the English-speaking community and a list of religious services in English. It also provides good coverage of national and international news. On the internet there is a site at www.chip.cl with daily news from Chile translated into English. There is a German language Chilean newspaper called *Wochenshau Chile der Zeitung CONDOR*. A number of foreign language newspapers and magazines can be found at kiosks in the downtown area of Santiago.

Television

Cable television in Chile is very good. You can receive Latin American, European and American channels for a fee. CNN has a Spanish language station in addition to its regular English broadcast. Chilean television offers a wide array of local programs, dubbed foreign language shows and movies. Important television hosts in Chile include Cesar Antonio Santis, Antonio Vodanovic and Cecilia Bolocco, former Miss Universe.

Telenovelas

A cultural phenomenon common throughout Latin America is the soap opera or *telenovela*. Literally everyone watches the *telenovelas*. Foreigners are often shocked by how good they are, given the poor quality of such fare available in many other countries. Even Chilean men avidly watch them, and they are a topic of casual conversation among family members or good friends. Latin American *telenovelas* only last about five months, after which time they end and rarely have a sequel, allowing the actors to pursue other shows. The actors are household names in Latin America, and appear in many different *telenovelas*, so you will get to know them if you live in Chile for any length of time.

At first all the *telenovelas* will seem the same to you. But after a time you can distinguish the imports – from Mexico, Venezuela, Argentina and Brazil – from the local shows. If you are not well integrated into Chilean society it may be the best way for you to observe Chileans. However, as there is much talk and very little action, they may be hard to follow until your Spanish is very good. Chilean *telenovelas* are usually filmed in neighborhoods around Santiago, places that you know. Recently some Chilean *telenovelas* have explored such modern topics as unwed mothers and AIDS.

Sábado Gigante

The Chilean television program that has become an institution throughout the Americas is called *Sábado Gigante*, or Giant Saturday. As the name implies, it is long, almost seven hours – from 1:30 p.m. to 8:15 p.m. every Saturday. A live audience participates in contests and watches skits, interviews and news reports. Don Francisco is the popular host of the show and has been on *Sábado Gigante* for 25 years. His real name is Mario Kreutzberger, but everyone calls him by his stage name. In the last few years he has been dividing his week between Santiago and Miami, where he tapes a version of the show seen in practically every country in North and South America. Chileans are very proud of the fact that *Sábado Gigante* originated in Chile and is now the most widely watched show in all of Latin America. As Don Francisco says every week, Latinos are "Separados por la distancia, unidos por el idioma." One feels the sense of Latin American unity watching his program.

Cinema

Movies are popular in Chile, although the great majority are imported. There is some government censorship of movies in Chile. Movies are reviewed and rated and if necessary banned. "The Last Temptation of Christ" was banned from the country, which shows the strong influence of the church. However, a much more common and curious phenomenon is the practice of self-censorship. Many distributors will shamelessly cut their own movies in order to receive a lower rating, allowing the film to be seen by a wider audience. It might be better to wait until returning home to see a controversial movie.

Movies are not dubbed (to the everlasting thanks of the expatriates), but have subtitles, except for children's animated movies. In Santiago you can find other original language films in Italian and French. You must remember that in Chile seats are assigned in the cinema. You choose your seat when you buy the ticket. Tickets are half price on Wednesday. As a result, many shows are sold out, so if you want to take advantage of the bargain, buy your tickets either Tuesday or Wednesday morning. Many foreigners complain that the sound quality is not very good in the older theaters; perhaps because Chileans read the subtitles they do not mind.

There are many video clubs in Chile, but remember that the Spanish movie titles are not always translated literally from the original title. Sometimes the Spanish title is very different, and we recommend you ask for films by actor if you are having problems locating a movie.

SPORTS

At the international level, Chile is not well-known for sports. But all Chileans have enjoyed a few shining moments, such as third place in the 1962 World Cup soccer tournament hosted by Chile, the Davis Cup final and a few Olympic metals. Marlene Ahrens is well-known in Chile for being one of the greatest javelin throwers.

In Chile you can find many sports facilities, although the prices are prohibitive for many. Sports such as tennis and golf are generally reserved for the upper classes. Tennis is a favorite as from time to time Chile produces top rate players. Anita Lizana won a cup at Wimbledon and Marcelo "El Chino" Ríos is currently a top seeded men's player.

Chile has fine horseback riders, as there is a large enough upper class to support the sport, and the national team usually does well at the Olympics. A Chilean rider, Alberto Larraguibel (now deceased) holds the international high jumping record for horses. Horse racing is a more popular spectator sport, with fine Chilean horses appearing at tracks around the world. The two main racing events each year are the Derby in Viña del Mar in January and El Ensayo in Santiago in October.

While on the topic of animal sports, it should be mentioned that although many have the impression that cockfighting is popular in Latin America it is illegal in Chile and not common. The same applies to bull fighting which was banned in the 19th century.

Skiing

Skiing in Chile offers challenging slopes which are well groomed with good chairlifts. Most ski resorts are above the tree line and offer a unique panorama. Some resorts even have a sea view! Ski season is from June to September or October. There are 14 ski centers in Chile, and the number is expanding. The most important resorts are Portillo, 160 kilometers (100 miles) from Santiago, and the Farellones-La Parva-Valle Nevado complex only 50 kilometers (31 miles).

Basketball

Basketball is very popular in southern Chile because it can be played indoors during the long, wet winter. Chile even imports basketball players from other countries, and the Chileans themselves generally do well at Latin American basketball tournaments.

Soccer

Latin America is very famous for its soccer teams. Of course, Chile is not one of the big names like Argentina or Brazil; nevertheless, the level of play is very high. "Matador" Salas and "Bam Bam" Zamorano are local and international heroes. Soccer is called *fútbol* in Spanish. Every city or mid-sized town has a professional soccer team, but there is a large gap between the big clubs who pay their players very high salaries and have great facilities and the smaller clubs who have much tighter budgets.

TRIGG

Soccer games are indeed an event complete with fireworks and giant flags. Chilean soccer fans are very enthusiastic and the stadiums are full an hour and a half before the game. While there is no major gang problem in Chile, some gangs do exist based upon soccer supporters. At games the fans wear the colors of their team and sit in specific sections of the stadium. You should be aware that fights and violence can erupt when fierce rivals play one another. So do not be surprised to see lots of policemen at a soccer game.

Soccer has an official season that runs from March through December. There are two major championships – the Opening Championship (Campeonato de Apetura) and the Official Championship. Matches are usually held on Saturday and Sunday, occasionally on Wednesday, generally at 4:00 p.m.

Children's Games

If your children have Chilean friends or attend a Chilean school you may be surprised by the new games they learn. Of course, Chilean children play many games that are common to all cultures, such as *bolitas* (marbles), *luche* (hopscotch), checkers, jump rope, roller skates and kites. Some of the Chilean games originated abroad. *Palo ensebado* (the greased pole) originated in Italy where it is called *cucana*. A tall pole is driven into the ground and lubricated with soap or grease. Children try to climb to the top of the pole to reach prizes. *Rayuela* is a coin pitch game that originated in Spain. Disks or coins are thrown to a line drawn on the ground. The player who gets closest to the line wins the other players' coins. Another adult game is *Cacho*, a dice game played by rolling the dice in a cup-shaped piece of leather. It is a favorite drinking game.

NIGHTLIFE

In Santiago there are several very good nightlife spots. As Chile is a somewhat stratified society, the hotspots are frequented by a certain type of clientele, which may change over the years. A familiar neighborhood is Bellavista, a trendy, bohemian area with restaurants, discos and bars, some with live bands. The Suecia area in Providencia offers much of the same and is expanding as yuppies, both Chilean and foreign, increasingly hang out there. In the past Providencia was very *cuico*, but recently the patrons have started frequenting the more fashionable El Bosque Norte area instead.

There are discos in Santiago for many different ages and music tastes. You may have to be a night owl to put on your dancing shoes since discos open around midnight and stay open till 5:00 a.m.! Discos are frequented mostly by couples, but there are lots of single men, and it is fine for single women to go in groups. There are huge discos hidden on the outskirts of Santiago, which poses a problem because of drunk driving. The more underground, cutting edge discos are in industrial areas or warehouses and you need to know the right people to find out the locations.

HOTELS AND MOTELS

The difference between a hotel and motel in Chile and most of Latin America is not so simple. A hotel is a hotel, but a motel – unless clearly marked "motel de turismo" – is strictly for lovers. Motels used to be a place where couples having adulterous affairs could go. It is quite a fascinating set-up. Upon entering a motel in your car, you see no one and no one sees you. A voice tells you which room is yours and the door is opened. You pay through a slit in the wall. After parking, your car is hidden by a huge curtain so that other patrons will not recognize it. Some motels are merely rooms, but others have hot tubs, heart-shaped beds, porn flicks, etc. Young couples who live at home and have nowhere else to go make up the biggest market for motels, along with married Latin lovers getting something on the side.

In Santiago the most famous and expensive motel is the Valdivia downtown. It is customary for newlyweds to go there for their honeymoon. Motels are openly recognized for what they are and are used as landmarks. Laura once lived two houses away from a motel, and everyone, from old ladies to children, knew where it was. Of course most raised their eyebrows and joked about her being able to see whose cars went in and out.

Make sure you know the difference between a hotel and a motel!

191

Many Santiaguinos escape to the nearby beaches on weekends.

WEEKEND GETAWAYS

Finally, there are many things to do in Chile for those who long to escape Santiago's pollution on the weekends or explore nearby. The beaches close to Santiago, such as Reñaca, El Quisco, Algarrobo and El Tabo, are the obvious choice, but check out the northern beaches which are quieter and have a longer season. In line with the conservative nature of the country, there are no nude or topless beaches. This does not mean, however, that you will not see any skimpy bikinis. A group of hippies congregates on the beach of Horcón, north of Viña del Mar.

There is horseback riding in the Santuario de la Naturaleza (nature sanctuary) at the base of the cordillera. Wineries which are not too far outside of Santiago can be toured much more extensively than in other wine-producing nations. Chileans will allow you to view every step of the wine-making process, which is especially interesting at harvest time. The Cajón del Maipo is nice for a Sunday drive from Santiago into the canyon. The Maipo River, which runs through the canyon, offers rafting close to home. *Huaso* rodeos are also a short distance from the capital. Free tourist information is available from SERNATUR (Servicio Nacional de Turismo). There are many branch offices located throughout the country. The main office is at Avenida Providencia 1550 (telephone: (56-2) 236-1430 and 236-1416) in the Providencia sector of Santiago.

Adventure Tourism

Adventure tourism is really taking off in Chile. You can trek in the Andes, climb a volcano, go white-water rafting, walk on a glacier or bungee jump from the Malleco bridge. An excellent system of national parks offers lots of camping and hiking, especially in the south. Be prepared to pay a high entrance or guide fee.

Accommodations

There are accommodations in Chile for all budgets. At the lower end are *hospedajes*, which are family homes with rooms for rent that normally include breakfast and a shared bathroom and sitting room. *Residencias* are small hotels, *pensiones* are a step up as they offer a private bath. At the top are hotels, both modest and luxurious. Many travel agencies in Santiago sell package tours for those who prefer the convenience.

Transportation

The train in Chile is slow and not very modern. Better options are to either fly or take a bus. There are a number of different bus classes. For long or overnight rides, the most expensive class offers wide seats that recline well over 45 degrees. The ride is very pleasant and is much cheaper than plane fare. The ticket includes beverages (both alcoholic and non-alcoholic), dinner and breakfast. There is a bus attendant who fulfills your every need and organizes games for the passengers. Movies are also shown on board. These buses normally leave in the evening and arrive early morning and surprisingly you arrive refreshed and ready to take on the day. *¡Buen viaje!*

— *Chapter Twelve* —

BEYOND THE CAPITAL

OUTSIDE SANTIAGO

Depending upon your line of work, there is a chance that you may not be living in Santiago. Many of those who work in the mining industry find themselves in northern Chile. Those involved in the forestry or fishing industries will most likely wind up in the southern part of the country. There are a number of vibrant cities in Chile besides Santiago and this chapter will provide you with a brief introduction to some of the largest and most important.

Arica

Arica, known as the "City of Eternal Spring," is an important shipping port for southern Peru and Bolivia (the only landlocked country in Latin America). Arica is linked by land and railway to Tacna (Peru) and Bolivia. Feria Maximo Lira, the local market, sells many items from across the border.

In the 1950s, Chilean President Ibáñez conferred Arica with the status of duty-free port. During the following decade several companies established plants in Arica to take advantage of the tax exemptions. During this time, the population increased and the infrastructure grew. With the introduction of a free-market economy in the 1970s and 1980s, Arica no longer enjoyed its privileged status. Currently the city depends upon international trade, fishing and tourism, and is a major supplier of fishmeal, used for animal feed.

It rarely rains in Arica, but it is somewhat humid. The average temperature is 20°C (68°F). However, temperature variations during the day can be extreme, ranging from 0–40°C (32–104°F).

Iquique

Iquique, once the center of the saltpeter (nitrate) industry, is now famous for its Duty Free Zone, ZOFRI. Within ZOFRI goods are exempted from import duties and value added tax (VAT) as long as purchases are clearly for personal consumption.

Iquique is Chile's main fishing port. Most of the catch is used to produce fish oil and fishmeal. Other important industries are manufacturing, agriculture and mining.

A recent study conducted by *Qué Pasa* magazine rated Iquique one of the top three most habitable cities. A fair number of expatriates do live here. Primary and secondary education is ranked among the best, but there is only one university. Health care is reliable and the cost of living is low. There is very little traffic congestion in spite of the fact that the city has the highest number of cars per capita in the country. There are some restaurants, pubs and discos, museums and a cinema. However, it should be noted that the crime rate in Iquique is among the worst in the country, due mainly to high levels of drug addiction.

Antofagasta

Antofagasta is Chile's fourth largest city and capital of the II Region. The city is heavily reliant upon the mining industry. In fact, mining accounts for half of the gross regional product. It is the major city of the north and one of Chile's most important shipping ports. Chuquicamata, Chile's largest copper mine, other large copper mines, such as La Escondida, and saltpeter, lithium, borax and phosphorus mines are located here. The fishing industry is also important.

Antofagasta was rated one of the top five cities in which to live. There are three universities and the level of health care is very high. However, here too the crime rate and drug use levels are high by Chilean standards. There are a number of restaurants and pubs, but culturally speaking, Antofagasta does not have much to offer. There are some good beaches. Antofagasta is located near the driest desert in the world, and it is here that many tourists begin their forays into the Atacama Desert to see the Valle de la Luna, the Tatio geysers, the Atacama salt flat, the nitrate mines and the picturesque town of San Pedro de Atacama.

La Serena

A beautiful city noted for its architecture, La Serena was recently rated the number one city in Chile. The second oldest city in the country, it grew exponentially during the mining boom, fueled primarily by the silver and copper industries. More recently, however, agriculture (mainly fruit), nearby astronomical observatories, mining and tourism have been responsible for the city's economic growth.

Nearly one third of this region's population is involved in agriculture. Fruit, vineyards and new agro-industries dominate this region's economy. Most Chilean *pisco* (a distilled alcohol made from white grapes) comes from this area, specifically the Elqui Valley.

La Serena headed the list of most livable cities due to the relatively low crime rate. There are highly rated schools and universities and the cost of living is relatively low. There are a number of restaurants, museums, theaters, art galleries, libraries, book stores and every year the city celebrates the Silent Movie Festival (Festival de Cine Mudo). A short drive to the town of Vicuña will take you to the home and museum of Chile's Nobel laureate, Gabriela Mistral.

The skies in this part of the country are among the clearest and driest in the world which has made this zone the main astronomical observation center in the Southern Hemisphere. El Tololo Inter-American Observatory is run by the National Optical Astronomical Observatory, an association of American universities and the Universidad de Chile. La Silla Observatory is administered by the European Southern Observatory, made up of seven European countries, and Las Campanas Observatory is operated by the Carnegie Institute in Washington, D.C.

Viña del Mar and Valparaíso

These twin cities constitute the second largest metropolitan area after Santiago. Viña, heavily reliant on tourism, and Valparaíso, a picturesque port, lie about 120 kilometers (72 miles) northwest of Santiago.

Valparaíso, the country's main port, houses Chile's naval headquarters and the seat of Congress. In the early 19th century, with the rise of world trade and well before the construction of the Panama Canal, Valparaíso was a re-supply station for boats coming from Europe and the United States. Goods unloaded here were reshipped to other ports in the Pacific and Oceania. During this time, many British, French and Germans settled in Valparaíso. The British came not only to work in the trade industry, but also as technical advisers to the Chilean navy. A strong British influence can still be felt today.

Once the financial and commercial center of Chile, the city later experienced a decline. In an attempt at a revival, the military government relocated Congress to Valparaíso in the mid-1980s, but the move has not had the desired effect. Santiaguinos have not been enticed to relocate or establish businesses here and, in fact, Congressmen maintain homes in Viña and/or return to Santiago daily. One negative side effect has been an increase in the number of car accidents as the members of Congress rush back and forth from Santiago in order to make meetings.

This does not mean, however, that the city is dull. Quite the contrary, Valparaíso has a great deal of character. Although the Chilean film industry produces only a handful of movies each year, the majority are filmed here because of its beauty, mystery and charm. Funiculars, called *ascensores*, are located throughout the city, carrying people to and from their homes high on the hills. A ride up any funicular will treat you to spectacular views, both during the day and evening. On Sundays, a huge market, selling everything from fruits and vegetables, to furniture and baby chicks, enlivens the city. The nightlife includes numerous pubs, discos and restaurants. Chile's best technical university, Santa María University, is also located here.

There is also a seedy side to the city, due in part to the fact that it is a port of call for many sailors. Prostitution is widespread. Crime is a serious problem in Valparaíso. If you wander about Valparaíso be careful to stay in well-populated areas and beware of pickpockets.

Viña del Mar, once a private *hacienda*, began as a tourist resort for Santiaguinos and the nearby residents of Valparaíso. Viña offered beautiful beaches and ample land for building huge summer residences. Much of the growth in the "Garden City" is quite recent, as new high-rise apartment buildings have sprung up throughout the city to cater to the growing number of Santiaguinos coming here. The infrastructure is well-suited to handle tourism and there are many restaurants, hotels, shopping areas and discos. There are also theaters, art galleries, libraries and the main strip in downtown Viña comes alive at night with locals, Santiaguinos, tourists, street performers and artisans. Viña also boasts a large casino. Go to Viña just to relax; it's a great escape from the cold, pollution and hectic pace of Santiago.

Viña was rated the second most desirable city in Chile. The quality of education offered in the city's schools are well above the national average and the level of health care is among the best. Quality of life, especially in terms of climate, is very good.

San Antonio

Just south of Valparaíso is another main shipping port, San Antonio. Activity at this port is rapidly growing, taking some business away from Valparaíso. The town itself is a typical port town, full of working class Chileans. It is well known for its great seafood market, but does not have much else to offer. Explore the little seaside towns near San Antonio.

Concepción

Founded in 1550, Concepción was destroyed by the earthquake and tsunami of 1751. The capital of the VIII Region was rebuilt in 1764 at its present location. This region is Chile's second most populous

The entire Pacific coastline is dotted with cozy little towns, perfect for a relaxing weekend.

and is an agricultural and industrial center. Wheat, wine, and coal are produced here and the forestry industry also plays a very important role. In the late 19th century the forests in this area were clear-cut in order to grow wheat to feed workers. Unfortunately, this led to land erosion and currently reforestation projects have been implemented using Radiata pine. About 65 percent of the country's pine plantations are located in this region.

The Lota coal mine, once the largest coal mine in Chile, was located just south of Concepción. Coal mining began in 1852 and the money-losing mine was finally closed down in 1997 amidst major protests. This is undoubtedly one of the poorest regions of Chile and many people lost their jobs when the mine was closed.

The University of Concepción is well-known and highly respected throughout the country. It is the only true university campus in Chile. There are also five other universities located here. Because it is a populous city there are a number of restaurants, theaters, pubs and discos. From Concepción southwards, the temperature gradually decreases and rainfall levels increase. Temperatures during winter range from 0–13°C (32–55°F) and from 15–35°C (59–95°F) in the summer. There is heavy rainfall during the winter months.

Nearby is the Bío Bío River where adventure tourists travel to ride the grade five rapids. Sadly, a series of dams is under construction and parts of the river will no longer to accessible to white-water rafting.

Temuco

Temuco began as a fortress designed to defend early settlers from attacks by the Mapuche. Today, Temuco is the fastest growing city in Chile. The boom is centered around the agricultural and forestry industries. The area surrounding Temuco is home to many of the indigenous people of Chile. The region is referred to as La Frontera, the frontier, because for so many years the Mapuche were able to repel various advances and resist domination. In spite of the fact that

Temuco is experiencing high levels of growth, the native people remain impoverished.

The most important tourist attractions in Temuco are the craft and produce market where the Mapuche sell their wares. The museum and university are both well respected and a drive into rural areas offers views of traditional Mapuche houses and spectacular scenery. Temuco is also proud of its favorite son, Pablo Neruda, who incorporated this beautiful landscape and the perennial rainfall into many of his early poems.

Valdivia

Although the government did not offer free land to homestead in this part of Chile, many Germans still migrated to Valdivia. Using their own capital, the German population invested in industry and farming, and at the turn of the century Valdivia was Chile's leading industrial city. Today, many of the farms have become highly mechanized, producing a variety of crops. The dairy and forestry industries also play a major role in the economy.

A trip to the forts built by the Spanish at Corral, Niebla and Isla Mancera is a must. The fortresses date from the 17th century and were built at the mouth of the Calle Calle River, which links the Pacific Ocean to Valdivia. There is a very interesting museum on Isla Teja which has a beautiful collection of furniture and other items from the days of German immigration. Also, located on the Universidad Austral campus is a serene botanical garden and arboretum worth a lengthy stroll.

Puerto Montt and Puerto Varas

The Chilean government, frustrated in its attempts to colonize the southern part of the country and bring the Mapuche under control, initiated a program to actively recruit German settlers. In 1852 the first 212 German settlers arrived at Puerto Montt. They initially

Old houses, reminiscent of Victorian and German architecture, can be found throughout central and southern Chile.

inhabited the lake shores, transforming the area by clearing the dense temperate rainforest. Each German settler received 75 "blocks" of land (each slightly larger than a hectare) plus 12 "blocks" for each child. The families received free lodging until the land was handed over, a pair of oxen, one cow and calf, and boards and nails to build a house. They also received a monthly allowance for one year, free medical care, a certificate of ownership and Chilean citizenship, if they desired. The government ended the program in 1880.

Today Puerto Montt and Puerto Varas, combined with the city of Osorno, constitute Chile's fourth largest industrial center, with an economy based primarily on agriculture, including livestock, grains, potatoes, a variety of berries, and asparagus. Most of the milk consumed in Chile comes from here. There are more than 30 salmon farms in the area. The Lake District, as this region is known, is a major destination for national and international tourists.

The small fishing cove of Angelmó, part of the city of Puerto Montt, is famous for its seafood market. There is an unlimited variety of fresh seafood that ranges from *lenguado* (flounder) to *erizos* (sea urchin) and *picorocos*. *Picorocos* live in tube-like shells clustered together in colonies that resemble a rock. In the market you will see their beaks sticking out from the tubes. The Chilean way of eating *picorocos* is to grab the beak, pull the *picoroco* out and swallow it raw. Some delicacies are only for the adventurous.

Puerto Montt is also the main port for boats traveling south. Most of the cruises to the Laguna San Rafael and various small towns originate here. The Laguna San Rafael is a lake at the tip of a fjord which boasts a breathtaking glacier. The lake is dotted with small boats, full of tourists drinking whiskey "on the rocks," i.e., poured over million-year-old pieces of ice from the glacier. Depending upon the itinerary, it takes about two days to reach the laguna. More expensive and luxurious boats make stops at picturesque fishing towns and hot springs.

Punta Arenas

The most important city on the southern tip of the country, Punta Arenas, lies on the Straits of Magellan. In fact, this was the first part of Chile seen by Europeans. The earliest settlers of Punta Arenas were involved in sheep farming. Subsequent arrivals were tempted by the rumors of vast gold deposits in the area. The rumors proved to be false.

Before the Panama Canal was completed, Punta Arenas was the only port in the Straits of Magellan. All ships en route from Europe to the Pacific Coast passed through here. Later migrants sought a living working in the oil wells. The current economy is based on cattle, mining and fishing. Punta Arenas is also the gateway to the Chilean Antarctic Territory.

Punta Arenas is part of Chilean Patagonia and as such has lured adventurers and mavericks. Considered a wild frontier, Patagonia was populated by people from many different countries. A great many people in Punta Arenas are of Croatian origin. A sampling of surnames in this region is proof of the great tide of immigration.

Relations between southern Chile and southern Argentina are close due to cross-border traffic of goods and people. Although the two countries have had border disputes, the people of Patagonia are more closely connected to each other than to their fellow citizens in Santiago and Buenos Aires.

Punta Arenas was rated one of the top five cities in which to live. The quality of education in the primary and secondary schools is very high and the crime rate is low. However, the cost of living is as high as in Santiago given that supplies must be flown in. Also, airfare to and from Santiago is relatively expensive. The city does not have much to offer by way of cultural activities.

Punta Arenas is the beginning point for any trip to Torres del Paine, the cave of the Milodon or Tierra del Fuego. Torres del Paine is a pristine and untouched national park, with a variety of wild animals, such as *ñandues* and *guanacos*. Part of the reason this park remains unspoiled is because of the lack of infrastructure. To really experience this park you need to do some hiking. A 10-day trail circles the park, but it can only be completed during the summer months by knowledgeable hikers. There is also a boat (it only sails if the winds are not too strong) which brings you to a refuge (a building with a kitchen and bunk beds) from which you can do day hikes. The mountains, glaciers and lakes are breathtaking and the wind is strong enough to uproot tents.

The climate in this entire region is influenced by its latitude (51–56°), the ocean, which moderates temperatures, and the strong winds which come off the Pacific Ocean. While temperatures during the summer months may reach 13°C (55°F), they can drop to below freezing in the winter. Average rainfall in this region is relatively low compared to the Central Valley and Lake District.

CULTURAL QUIZ

SITUATION ONE

You are a businessperson who studied in Chile. You have an appointment with a local Chilean firm and you are delighted to encounter an old school friend who is now a manager at the firm. Your appointment is actually with your friend's superior, who is a good deal older than you. Later, your friend invites you home to meet his spouse, children and parents, who all live together. At dinner you are served by the maid, who is an excellent cook, and you compliment her cooking abilities.

Should you use *tú* or *Usted* with the a) friend b) superior c) spouse d) children e) parents f) maid?

Comments

Your friend should be addressed as *tú*, as you probably began the relationship on that basis when you were students, and you are approximately the same age.

Since you have never met your friend's superior before, *Usted* would be used. The superior is also in a high position, is older, and the pretext for the conversation is business, all reasons to use *Usted*.

The spouse should be addressed as *tú*. Even though you have not met before, the spouse is married to your friend.

The children should be addressed as *tú*, as they are a great deal younger than you.

The parents of your friend would be addressed as *Usted*. You have never met them before and they are older. Even if you were the same approximate age as the parents, it would be best to use *Usted* because your connection to them is through their child.

The maid should be addressed as *Usted*. Anyone in service positions should be treated with the respect that *Usted* implies.

Remember that the children will probably use *Usted* with you, and the parents will probably use *tú*, even though you will use the opposite with them. This does not mean that you should change the form used. Only the parents, perhaps, after a time, will invite you to *tutear,* effectively acknowledging that you are equals. The invitation can only be extended by the superior, and should not be extended to children or servants.

SITUATION TWO

You are invited to a party at a Chilean's house. There are around 20 people there when you arrive. You only know five of these people, including the host. As you first enter the room you:

A Go immediately to the people you know, avoiding eye contact with the strangers, simply saying "Hello" to your friends.

B Greet the host, then work your way around the room slowly, kissing the right cheek of every person (if you are female), shaking hands with the males, and kissing the cheek of the females (if you are male).

C Go up to the host, thank him or her for inviting you, and expect the host to introduce you to the others.

Comments

If you were to act as in **A**, Chileans would think you very rude. Latinos make a lot of eye contact, so much so it seems at times like long-distance flirting or at least a good sizing-up. If you limit your contact to those whom you already know, it may insult the host, as he or she invited all the people whom they thought would get along well together. Of course, there will be some clustering among intimate friends, but at a large party one is expected to mingle. A verbal greeting is not sufficient in a social setting in Chile, cheek-kissing and shaking hands is the norm.

B is the correct choice. The host should be greeted first, but try and keep it brief to avoid monopolizing the host and losing your window of opportunity to introduce yourself. Chileans are not shy at parties, and they have no reservations about going up to complete strangers and introducing themselves. If you find someone really interesting to talk to while on this preliminary survey of the party, resist the temptation to stop and chat. Instead quickly finish introducing yourself to everyone and then return.

Chileans for the most part do not need a third party to introduce themselves to strangers in a social setting, as in **C**. Perhaps if you are a VIP, or speak no Spanish, the host will introduce you, but for the most part you are on your own.

SITUATION THREE

You run a red light and as a result have a minor car accident in Santiago. The Carabineros come and take your license. You should:

A Say repeatedly that you are a foreigner and they have no right to take away your license.

B Quietly take the Carabinero aside and offer him some pesos.

C Take the ticket and drive without your license until your court date.

Comments

A is an all too common response. However, the police in Chile do have the right to take your license if you have committed a minor violation. Just because the Chilean laws are not how you think they should be does not make you exempt from these laws. Some foreigners think that their passports give them unique legal status, but this is not the case.

B would work well in many Latin American countries, but not in Chile. It could get you into big trouble, so don't risk it.

C is the right answer. If you have any questions surrounding the correct procedure to get your license back you can call the offices of the municipality where the incident occurred.

SITUATION FOUR

After working for a few weeks in a Chilean office you go out for drinks with your co-workers. It comes out in the course of discussion that the majority of these Chileans are pro-Pinochet. You can:

A Get into a heated debate, citing the terrible human rights abuses committed under his regime.

B Listen to what they have to say and try and be non-judgmental.

C Ask who won the latest soccer game and change the subject.

Comments

A is most foreigners' gut response, but not a good choice given that around 40 percent of Chileans supported Pinochet when he stepped down, and many still admire the man today. It is hard to imagine what would allow Chileans to continue to back Pinochet. A full-blown verbal fight may feel like the right thing to do at the moment, but it will not change anyone's opinion. Plus your work life will probably be made miserable.

B is an option if your blood pressure can handle it. It is interesting to hear the other side in debates that seem to foreigners so one-sided. Laura once listened intently to a conversation giving all the benefits of Amazon deforestation. It did not change her opinion, but it was a learning experience.

If you are unable to keep calm for **B**, and want to stay out of trouble, then **C** is the best exit out of a thorny situation.

SITUATION FIVE

A close Chilean friend returns to Chile after living abroad for a year. You invite the friend over for *once*. Upon arrival, after the cheek kisses, your friend exclaims, "My God, how you have gained weight! You look so fat!" You can:

A Grimace, force back the tears, and tell your friend that you are considering liposuction.

B Glare and decide to never call this person again.

C Smile and remark on your friend's appearance.

Comments

A is a normal response to what seems like a very cutting comment. Chilean honesty in matters of appearance takes some getting accustomed to.

B would be a mistake, as this Chilean is not a bad person, just someone who has been raised in Chilean society, where cruel comments are not always meant to be so. Giving a false opinion of someone's appearance would, for a Chilean, be viewed as unnecessary. So take this remark as a sign of intimacy with your friend.

C is the best response, once you are able to go against your first instinct of being insulted.

SITUATION SIX

You become friendly with the landlady who owns your apartment. She obviously has some Mapuche or other Amerindian blood from her skin tone and features. You start talking about your upcoming trip to the Lake District. When you ask if anyone in her family still speaks Mapuche, the landlady becomes visibly offended, mutters an excuse, and leaves quickly. What happened?

    A The landlady hates the Mapuche.

    B The landlady is offended by a personal question.

    C The landlady is insulted that you consider her to be part Mapuche.

Comments

A is very unlikely. Most Chileans respect the Mapuche and consider them to be an important part of Chile, although disconnected from mainstream Chilean culture.

B is also unlikely, as Chileans have no problems answering questions about their family history and actually welcome your interest.

C is most likely the case. Although there was much mixing between the Amerindians and the Spanish in the early days of colonization, Chileans identify themselves as mainly of European descent because the dominant culture and language is European based. A much better question to pose to a Chilean is from which part of the world their ancestors came. This will please them, as it reinforces the accepted notion that Chile is a nation of immigrants.

SITUATION SEVEN

You are a businessperson who lives and works in Chile. You would like to do something nice for a Chilean business associate. You:

A Invite the Chilean for a round of golf at your club.

B Take the Chilean out to the night-clubs for a night of drinking.

C Invite the Chilean to your home for dinner.

Comments

A: While business smooching over a round of golf is common in many countries, Chile has not been caught up in the golfing craze. Most businesspeople do not play golf and it would be uncomfortable for someone to have to turn down your invitation because they don't know how to play. However, inviting the Chileans who are already members of your golf club to a round would be a perfect way to establish friendships.

B: Again, a night of free drinks is de riguer in many lands to cement a business relationship, but not particularly so in Chile. Some Chileans may take you up on your offer, but this behavior is not expected. In addition, it may not be the exact image you want to project. Others will politely refuse your invitation. If you insist, you may come off as annoying.

The best choice is **C**. A quiet dinner in your home is the perfect way to socialize with any Chilean, and is an important part of doing business in Chile. While the reputation of your company obviously matters, Chileans like to think that they are doing business with individuals, not just nameless representatives. It is much better to establish these close friendships as the Chileans do, in their homes. Of course, while Chilean businesspeople do take people out to restaurants, it is preferable to eventually introduce your business associates to your family in your home.

SITUATION EIGHT

A single foreign woman friend has come to work in Chile. She meets a Chilean man and they begin the intense Chilean-style dating. You accompany the new couple to dinner and a show, and in the course of the evening you discover that the man is in his mid-30s yet lives at home with his parents, never worked until finishing his advanced degree and insists on seeing your woman friend every day. The next day your friend asks your opinion of her new boyfriend. What do you think?

A Obviously a psychopath. You tell your friend to run as fast as she can.

B Seems like a typical Chilean. You wish her happiness in the relationship.

Comments

While **A** may be many foreigners' initial impression, all of the above behaviors are typical in Chile and in no way indicate deviant conduct.

B is the appropriate response. It may be hard to swallow that the man is not a total loser, but he is only behaving as Chilean society would have good sons and male suitors conduct themselves. In many cultures, a man this age who lives at home would be considered strange. But in Chile a single man who has just entered the job market often stays on at home for the convenience of free food, laundry and cleaning. He feels no pressure to leave either from his family or society. Another important factor is the intensity of family bonds in

Chile, where even married children may choose to live with their parents. The possessiveness of *pololeando,* or dating, in Chile may appear extreme, but is considered normal in their culture. His desire to sec her and talk to her constantly is a typical expression of his fondness for her.

FURTHER READING

Politics

A Nation of Enemies: Chile under Pinochet by Pamela Constable and Arturo Valenzuela (W.W. Norton and Company, NY: 1991).

An excellent and easy to read explanation and analysis of the breakdown of democracy in Chile.

Tapestries of Hope, Threads of Love: The Arpillera Movement in Chile 1974–1994 by Marjorie Agosin (University of New Mexico Press: 1996).

During the military dictatorship women who had lost members of their families used tapestries to tell their stories. Each *arpillera* became a strong form of protest. Agosin compiles interviews and pictures to provide the reader with an in-depth look into these women's lives. Her earlier book, *Scraps of Life, Chilean Arpilleras: Chilean Women and the Pinochet Dictatorship* (1987) also deals with this topic.

Chile: Death in the South by Jacobo Timerman (Knopf, NY: 1987)

A book on the brutal human rights abuses suffered in Chile under the military dictatorship.

Out of the Ashes: Life, Death and Transfiguration of Democracy in Chile, 1883-1988 by James R. Whelan (Regnery Gateway, Washington, D.C.: 1989).

This is for those who wish to gain an understanding of the pro-Pinochet point of view. Written by a foreigner, this book combines an economic and political analysis of Chilean history.

Business

Welcome to Chile published by the American Chamber of Commerce.
Valuable information on living and conducting business in Chile. Lots of helpful hints on how to settle down.

Doing Business in Chile: The Price Waterhouse Guide.
More valuable information for those in Chile on business.

Guide to the Chilean Business Environment: Trends 1997-1998 by Rafael Aldunate. (Inversiones Divisas Limitada, Santiago)
This guide is privately published in Santiago and contains information on social, economic and political elements of doing business in Chile. It also addresses the main sectors of the economy, explains the regulatory framework and describes selected corporations.

Travel and Tourism

Chile: A Remote Corner on Earth (Turismo y Comunicaciones S.A., Santiago).
By far the most comprehensive and detailed travel guidebook on Chile. A must for anyone who plans on staying in Chile for any length of time. The English version is sold as one book with a companion guide on adventure tourism. The Spanish version is published in four volumes. It is available in most large bookstores in Santiago and is known as the Turistel.

Chile and Easter Island, A Lonely Planet Travel Survival Kit.
A good guidebook for those who want to see as much as possible of Chile, but have a limited budget.

Chile, Insight Guides.
Much more than a travel guide, this book provides detailed information on Chilean culture. The beautiful pictures show just how much there is to see and do in Chile.

In Patagonia by Bruce Chatwin (Penguin Books, NY: 1977).

An interesting look at the harsh life experienced by settlers in Patagonia. Full of interesting stories and legends; a real treat.

South America's National Parks: A Visitor's Guide by William C. Leitch (The Mountaineers, Seattle: 1990).

A good reference book for those who plan on taking advantage of Chile's national parks.

Travels in a Thin Country: A Journey through Chile by Sara Wheeler (Abacus, London: 1994).

The Voyage of the "Beagle" by Charles Darwin (J.M. Dent and Sons Ltd., London: 1959).

For those who enjoy reading about old world travel and are interested in the development of Darwin's theories.

Culture and Folklore

Cultures of the World: Chile by Jane Kohen Winter (Times Books International, Singapore).

A wonderful introduction to Chilean culture with some spectacular photos.

Mapuche: Seeds of the Chilean Soul. (Port of History Museum, Philadelphia, PA, USA and the Museo Chileno de Arte Precolombino, 1992).

An excellent book on the Mapuche, their beliefs, traditions and crafts. One of the very few books available in English on the Mapuche, it can be found at the Pre-Columbian Museum in Santiago.

Easter Island: Archaeology, Ecology and Culture by Jo Anne Van Tilburg (Smithsonian Institute, 1995).

Van Tilburg, an archaeologist who has spent over 12 years doing research on Easter Island, uses recently acquired information to examine the myths and folklore of Rapa Nui. This book by the foremost authority on Easter Island should not be missed by anyone interested in the history of the island.

Easter Island: Mystery of the Stone Giants by Catherine Orliac and Michel Orliac (Harry N. Abrams Pub.: 1995).

Translated from the French by Paul G. Bahn, this concise book is packed with interesting information.

Language

How to Survive in the Chilean Jungle by John Brennan and Alvaro Taboada (Chilean-North American Institute, Santiago: 1996).

A fun and complete guide to Chilean slang. A must for those who wish to speak Chileno. This book can be found in stores in Chile.

Fiction

The House of Spirits by Isabel Allende.

A captivating story about a Chilean aristocratic family interwoven with historical events.

Memoirs by Pablo Neruda.

The poet's autobiography written in the form of beautiful short pieces.

Twenty Love Poems and a Song of Despair by Pablo Neruda.

The best-known and best-loved collection of Neruda's early work. It predates his political days and is simply and beautifully an exaltation of love.

Persona Non-Grata: A Memoir of Disenchantment with the Cuban Revolution by Jorge Edwards (Paragon House).

Although the story takes place primarily during the author's days in Cuba, it does reflect to a large degree Chilean social and political life.

A House in the Country by José Donoso.

This story revolves around a house where the children are in charge, following the departure of the adults. It is a metaphor for the transformation of Chilean society from one which treasured old, traditional values to a younger, more modern society.

This Sunday by José Donoso.

This collection of short stories is in reality a critique of Chilean society.

Clandestine in Chile: The Adventures of Miguel Littin by Gabriel García Márquez (H. Holt, NY: 1987).

Miguel Littin is the best-known Chilean cinematographer. He was forced into exile, but returned illegally during the military dictatorship to make a documentary. García Márquez, famous for his fiction, reverts to his origins as a journalist to recount Littin's experiences.

Websites

www.brujula.cl

A great website for exploring the many aspects of life in Chile. The *brujula*, which means compass, can lead you to other websites on the topics of media, government, education, economy, health, tourism, business, organizations, entertainment, etc. Many of the websites are in Spanish, but there are some in English. German speakers can access the German language Chilean newspaper *Wochenshau Chile der Zeitung CONDOR* through the *brujula* website.

www.chile.cl

This website is another good introduction to general information on Chile, particularly the government, economy, climate, tourism, etc. There is a Spanish and an English version.

www.chip.cl

Chip news offers the English translation of several top news stories in the country on a daily basis. More than merely translating, the site also provides background information on particularly involved stories. Great for those who wish to keep abreast of recent happenings.

www.tmm.cl/corfo/

CORFO, the Chilean Economic Development Corporation (a government agency), provides very good information on the Chilean economy through this website.

www.minrel.cl

This is the official website of the Ministry of Foreign Relations. Most of the information is in Spanish, but the embassies in Australia, New Zealand, South Africa and Norway have their own pages in English.

THE AUTHORS

Susan Roraff was born in Chicago, Illinois. She received her Masters degree in Latin American Studies from Georgetown University. Following graduation, she worked at the Latin American program of the Woodrow Wilson International Center for Scholars in Washington, D.C. She then moved to Santiago, Chile where she lived for two years, working at an economics research organization and later in conference planning. It was during this time that she met her Chilean husband and traveled extensively throughout Latin America. She has also lived in Vienna, Austria, and Singapore.

Laura Camacho, a native of Galena, Illinois, was a Rotary exchange student to Bolivia. She later married a Latin American and studied Psychology at the Catholic University in La Paz, Bolivia for three years. She received a Bachelor of Arts in Psychology and Spanish and a Master's degree in Spanish Literature and Linguistics from the University of Wisconsin-Madison. Laura has lived the expatriate life on four continents, but her heart remains in Latin America.

ACKNOWLEDGEMENTS

The authors recognize that this book would not have been possible without the assistance of many people. Our heartfelt thanks go to those who read and re-read the manuscript: Laura Mullahy, Peter Siavelis, Carol and Robert Roraff, Brian Roraff, Ray Harris, Barbara and James Darling and Amy Darling-True. Their comments and corrections were invaluable. We would also like to thank Katty Kauffman, Vanessa Chan, Gary Bland, Lynda Grahill, Reinhard and Helga Steinmeyer, Jill Kugenheim, Vanessa Friedman, Jason Kempen, Matt Meyers, Joseph Thome, Krista Schneph, Jeff Wing and Ron Leiden for sharing their experiences and culture shock while they lived in Chile. Thanks also to the many Chileans who so eagerly explained Chilean society and made us feel so welcome in their country. Of course, any errors are the sole responsibility of the authors.

INDEX